"As John Lennon said, 'Life is what happens when you're busy making other plans.'

Wendi Lou Lee's Red Tail Feathers offers a new way of looking at the things that happen to us when real life intrudes on our seemingly well made plans. She explains that 'grief has its own trajectory.' Her stories show that love, happiness and even the concept of family, clearly have theirs as well. No stranger to the hardest parts of life, she speaks from her own experience and describes her personal journey to finding her own understanding of grace.

The day she woke up from brain surgery, a healthcare worker told her that she seemed as if her 'veins were full of liquid joy.' This is an excellent description of Wendi and the way in which she shares her gifts with the world."

—ALISON ARNGRIM, NELLIE OLESON FROM *LITTLE HOUSE ON THE PRAIRIE* AND NY TIMES BESTSELLING AUTHOR

RED TAIL
FEATHERS

RED TAIL
FEATHERS

*Dare to Discover the
Beauty of Grace*

a memoir

WENDI LOU LEE

For information about this title or to order other books and/or electronic media, contact the publisher:

Pocketful of Sunshine, an imprint of Wendi Lou Lee
wendiloulee@gmail.com
https://wendiloulee.com

Scripture quotations are from The ESV® Bible (The Holy Bible, English Standard Version®), copyright © 2001 by Crossway, a publishing ministry of Good News Publishers. Used by permission. All rights reserved. Scripture quotations marked (AMPCE) are taken from the Amplified Bible, Copyright © 1954, 1958, 1962, 1964, 1965, 1987 by The Lockman Foundation. Used by permission.
Library of Congress Control Number: 2023907003

ISBN 979-8-9881684-0-9 (Hardcover)
ISBN 979-8-9881684-1-6 (Paperback)
ISBN 979-8-9881684-2-3 (Ebook)
ISBN 979-8-9881684-3-0 (Audio)

Printed in the United States of America.
Location Photos by Jackie Juchniewicz.
Book Design by Typewriter Creative Co.
Editing by Mick Silva and Nicole O'Meara.
Headshot by Sarah Smith.

Publisher's Cataloging-in-Publication data
Names: Lee, Wendi Lou, author.
Title: Red tail feathers : dare to discover the beauty of grace / Wendi Lou Lee.
Description: Arroyo Grande, CA: Pocketful of Sunshine, 2023.
Identifiers: LCCN: 2023907003 | ISBN: ISBN 979-8-9881684-0-9 (hardcover) | 979-8-9881684-1-6 (paperback) | 979-8-9881684-2-3 (ebook) | 979-8-9881684-3-0 (audio)
Subjects: LCSH Lee, Wendi Lou. | Motion picture actors and actresses--United States--Biography. | Child actors--United States. | Little house on the prairie (Television program) | Christian biography. | Christian living. | Christian women--Biography. | BISAC BIOGRAPHY & AUTO-BIOGRAPHY / Personal Memoirs | BIOGRAPHY & AUTOBIOGRAPHY / Entertainment & Performing Arts | RELIGION / Christian Living / Personal Memoirs | RELIGION / Christian Living / Inspirational | RELIGION / Christian Living / Women's Interests
Classification: LCC PN1998.2 .L44 2023 | DDC 791.43/028/092--dc23

For Brenda

You have been with me since the beginning,
and I wouldn't have it any other way.

Contents

————

Introduction

——

My husband, Josh, and I sat in silence in our car in the medical building parking lot. We had just received a positive report, so I was relieved, yet my husband's silence had left me confused and feeling misunderstood. On one hand, we both knew we had plenty of reasons to celebrate. We had survived the most difficult experience of our lives as a married couple. But the diagnosis, the surgery, and especially my transitioning back home had exposed insecurities in our relationship and pillaged us to the core. And for the first time, maybe ever, our fundamental perspectives about X didn't align. I was north and he was south. We weren't just on different pages, we were reading different books on opposite sides of the bookstore.

I stared through the front windshield and examined the stucco on the side of the building, desperately wishing that God would give me a revelation—a clue to solving the mess of emotions and to somehow turn it all around. I would have given anything for a redo of the past week. Coming home after surgery instigated all kinds of fears in me, but even more so in Josh. His grasping for control came across as rigid and sometimes unsympathetic. He didn't trust my post-brain-surgery decisions and had begun treating me as if I wasn't the same woman he married. I'd never felt so alone.

The words that toppled out of my mouth were meant to sting, a hasty challenge delivered at the worst possible moment. And my subsequent apology didn't fix anything, it had done its damage.

The bright blue sky stretched out above us and the subtle ocean breeze blew the palm trees ever so gently—a typical November day in Santa Barbara, California. A perfect day wasted. We'd sat in this parking lot the week before surgery with more hope than now. It didn't make any sense. How could I convince him that everything would be okay when he didn't trust me anymore?

He studied his folded hands. There was nothing left to say. I stared straight ahead praying for a glimmer of light to brighten the darkness closing in around us. Just then, right in front of our bumper, a pretty little tree in a square of dirt surrounded by cement caught my attention. Its leaves looked like emeralds dancing in and out of the branches. Thousands of them layered one upon the other.

"Where do you want to go from here?" Josh asked. It wasn't a question of where to go for lunch, and I didn't have an answer for him. I continued to stare out the window, mesmerized by the green light show. A war ensued inside my soul, while he checked his watch for the third time in five minutes. *What the heck does he expect me to say? I just had brain surgery for Pete's sake.*

A heavy sigh escaped my nostrils, and I kept avoiding his eyes. "What choice do we have? Life isn't going to get any easier. Not for a few months at least."

Suddenly, the green foliage fluttered, went still, then fluttered again. The branches created a cave-like den of protection from the wind. My eyes played tricks on me as I tried to focus, as if on a puzzle. Then two black, beady eyes stared back at me, resting on wings of dark green cloaked in the shade of the tree. A small bird, nearly invisible, perched on a twig, surrounded by natural camouflage, looking right at me. My eyes widened. I dropped my jaw and pointed through the windshield. "Can you see that?"

He squinted. "What am I looking at?"

"A bird. Can you see the bird in the tree?"

He leaned as far forward as the steering wheel allowed then relaxed. "You mean in that bush?"

"Whatever. You see it, right?" My eyes bounced back and forth between the tree and Josh's face.

"Yeah. Little thing was hiding from us this whole time. There's not much to him, is there?"

And then, our radiant green friend flew from the rustling canopy and landed on Josh's side mirror. Neither of us moved a muscle. Balanced on tiny legs, he moved in a continuous circular motion, like a toe-tapping supermodel strutting the catwalk.

As we watched in awe, a burst of fiery red flashed from the tips of its longest tail feathers. *Wowzers. How had I missed that?* It seemed stolen from an animated movie. One last stare-down through the window, and it flew off.

I felt embraced by the most subtle sensation of love. I leaned toward Josh, placing my hand gently on his arm and whispered, "I wonder if we're missing something … if the beauty of this moment is yet to be revealed."

Epiphanies tend to happen when I least expect them—my eyes suddenly see what they couldn't see before. The red tail feathers are often staring me in the face, but I'm not always ready to embrace their glory. Seldom am I patient enough to let the scene play out before drawing my conclusions, before giving up hope. That's the way grace works a lot of the time: unexpected beauty is obscured. I'm distracted by shrubbery. And there's a lot of shrubbery. Communication mishaps, disappointing the people we love, trying to live up to the expectations of those around us. If I'm not on the lookout for grace, I miss it completely.

The first time I connected a definition to the word grace was in Sunday school. An older gentleman volunteered to be our teacher. My leggy frame overwhelmed the too-small chairs arranged around a six-foot table of squirrely preteens. I had no reason to challenge his thinking, so I didn't. He read the definition with authority and told us to fill-in the blank on our worksheets. God's unmerited favor sounded like an intelligent concept, but my twelve-year-old self couldn't grasp what it meant. Getting what I didn't deserve was a tangled-up knot of an idea that I couldn't figure out how to untie. Even now I struggle to fully understand how it plays out in the real world.

I am truly grateful for forgiveness and salvation—gifts from God—I'm slowly learning that grace isn't about what we don't deserve, not entirely. It's about the heart of God.

God doesn't hand over a beautifully wrapped package and then list off all the reasons I don't deserve to receive it. He's not keeping track of my worthiness. Grace is about God's active involvement in my life. How He blesses me and surprises me with His generous gifts of love. It's how He wants to challenge and transform my faith through every unfortunate circumstance. Grace is so much more than a simple definition. It has as many meanings as there are good things on the earth, as many shades of paint as an artist can envision.

Did God send the bird as some kind of object lesson? I like to think so. That experience with the bird changed the way I respond and engage with the hard stories of my life. I was looking for something. The bird awakened me to the endless ways God chooses to demonstrate His grace.

When my eyes are open and looking for grace, I feel like I can see it in every personal interaction. In every beautiful sunset and every bird perched in a tree. The possibility of finding a sliver of goodness sends me searching for the evidence of it. And if I look hard enough, I believe I can always find it.

When my kids were little, we lived on a ranch with a pond full of bright orange salamanders. Even though they were easy to see, we'd miss them all the time. We had to train our eyes to spot them in the cracks and under the ledges where they liked to hide. If we didn't give up, the search would always end with a salamander in our hands. And that gave my kids a thrill.

But what about the painful aspects of life? If every action of God equals grace, then what about friends with cancer and divorce papers and racial injustice? What about forest fires and hurricanes? How could all of that be grace?

I honestly don't know. But I've seen grace sometimes hides itself in the hard moments, too. It doesn't always make a lot of sense to me, but then again, that's not unusual. I think God usually does His best work without me knowing about it. Maybe if I go looking for it more often, more diligently, I'll find it more. I won't pretend to know every answer. Life is beautiful, and in the same breath, more challenging than I can handle most days. Trusting God's goodness when our hearts are heavy is a complicated endeavor. But being open to what God is doing around us demands an openness of the mind and heart. It's the willingness to accept heartbreaking situations with honesty *and* anticipation of what God will reveal a little further down the line.

So here I am, pledging to do the hard work of searching for God's presence in the stories of my life. Gathering them together and taking a good hard look. Here I am opening my eyes to see the red tail feathers—of His grace. Collecting the evidence is like placing those salamanders in a mason jar and looking at them carefully. It's been a slow process of learning to understand how complex God is. How grace morphs and changes from what it first appeared to be. I'm discovering the reality of grace and why it matters.

The differing experiences of God's grace in my life show up in the most absurd ways. Ways I'll probably never fully understand. And that's okay. I just want to be willing to go on the search for more. Opening my eyes wide enough to notice. Eagerly accepting the dare to discover the beauty of grace all around us.

The only question for me now is, do I have the eyes to see His grace? Can I recognize the hidden beauty of God's activity in my life? Can I see beyond the dazzling emerald of shrubbery to the flash of red tail feathers? In the good and in the bad, in the insignificant and in the substantial. In my private moments and in my public moments. And then, do I have the courage to share my stories with a world searching for a little sunshine?

With eyes wide open, I just might see a red tail feather in every chapter of life.

My Girls on Television

Grace emerges from humble beginnings.

My six-month-old toddling self rolled around on a handmade quilt. The worn fabric shielded my baby-soft skin from the 70s brown shag carpet in our second-story apartment. The little dress I wore, edged with lace, hung over my cloth diaper protruding from the matching frilly bloomers. My twin sister, Brenda, clothed in the same outfit, rested on her stomach next to me, and my older sister, Michelle, sat in front of a pile of wooden blocks. In the corner of the living room, a portacrib acted as a makeshift napping station for when one of us turned cranky.

It was a typical day at home for my mom: constant diaper changes, feeding schedules, the endless cleaning up of toys and spit-up—not to mention washing enough cloth diapers for three little ones. To make life a little easier, my grandpa had rigged up a washer on the back patio with a hose running from the kitchen faucet so that Mom could keep an eye on us while the top loader did its magic. I imagine the song "Stayin Alive" by the Bee Gees playing in the background, Mom mouthing every word by heart. I don't know how she did it with a smile on her face. What I do know is that her life as a mother changed with one ring of the telephone.

She grabbed the receiver. "Hello." A rambling of excitement and information exploded from the voice on the other end. Mom pulled the handset away from her ear before answering in a slow calm voice.

"Hi, Mother. Yes, could you slow down? I can barely understand you."

My grandmother started her story again, but as she continued, her enthusiasm swelled like a river exceeding its banks and rushing through the center of town. The frenzy of emotions, the thrill to deliver this life-changing opportunity had her gasping for air—and eagerly hoping her daughter would agree.

"Interested? Well … of course, I'm interested. How couldn't I be?" My mom leaned against the kitchen counter, casually considering the plausibility of her mother's suggestion without hastily beginning to count imaginary chickens. Her palm cradled the side of her face, her eyes ablaze with too many questions.

"Yes, Mother. I'm still here." Mom struggled to grasp the reality of the conversation. "Okay, so let me get this straight. You showed a picture of the girls to Kent and now Michael Landon wants to meet them? This is unbelievable." A list of thoughts raced through my mother's head. *I'll have to talk it over with Dave, he'll need to be on board. I wonder what kind of money they pay babies to be on television? This could be fun, get me out of the house, and maybe make a couple extra bucks.* "Yes, Mother. I'll call Kent as soon as I talk it over with Dave. I'll call you back.… Bye."

After receiving a supportive, yet wary thumbs-up from my father, Mom clutched the phone again—this time with Kent McCray on the other end, the executive director of *Little House* and long-time friend of my grandparents. She hung up with all the details, still in disbelief. In her mind the whole scenario felt wild and exhilarating, maybe a fool's errand in the end, but why not? Meet Michael Landon. In person. She had never met an actor before, and definitely no one as well-known or handsome as Michael Landon.

A few days later, Mom packed a diaper bag and carried Brenda and me down the exterior stairwell of our apartment building. After loading us in her 1974 Ford Pinto, we made our way to Michael's office on the Paramount lot. A man in a dark blue uniform stood outside the security booth holding a clipboard. He scanned the list and opened the white gate arm with the push of a button while directing her toward a parking space.

As she pulled in, depressing the brake and moving the shift stick to park, her eyes caught a glimpse of Brenda and me in the rearview mirror. We each held a colorful plastic ring in our tiny grips, gnawing with contentment, the necks of our little dresses soaked in drool. My mom took a deep breath and tried to grasp the magnitude of this opportunity. If the meeting went well, her twin girls could be on television. She unbuckled our first-generation archaic car seats and hoisted one twin on her right hip and the other on her left, deciding against the enormity of the double stroller sitting in the trunk.

Through a set of glass double doors, a warm smile belonging to a lady in a white blouse greeted us from behind a desk. She pushed a button on the phone console and spoke into the receiver before leading us down the hall. She opened a door with the name "Michael Landon" etched in a gold frame and ushered my mom, still carrying a child on each hip, into the room. Two chairs stood between my mom and a huge wooden desk where Michael Landon waited to meet us.

Michael immediately stood up, flashing his bigger-than-life smile. My mom made her way across the room, not knowing what to do or say. I've heard from several cast members over the years that when Mike entered a room everything stopped.

The glow that surrounded him could fill a stadium. The same happened when he locked eyes with my mom and extended his hand from across the desk.

"It's so nice to meet you ... Jackie, right? And these are your twin girls?"

My mom nodded nervously as she lowered us to the rug between the two chairs and shook his hand. "Wendi and Brenda."

Michael's deep soulful eyes rested on my sister and me. He left his side of the desk and slowly slid to the floor, captivated by our every move: how we responded to a stranger's presence, our smiles and content personalities. After no more than five minutes, he stood up with a broad grin plastered on his charismatic face.

"These are my girls."

My mom's heart skipped a beat. Her eyes widened. *Did he just say 'my girls'? Wendi and Brenda ... Ingalls girls? I can't believe this is happening.*

"We start shooting Season 5 in a month. Kent will fill you in on the rest. Your girls are going to be the perfect Baby Grace Ingalls."

My mom gathered us up and walked to her car, buckled us in our car seats and drove home with one thought going through her head on repeat. *My girls, on television!*

The first glimmers of grace emerged that day in our second-story apartment and followed us into the meeting with Michael Landon. Looking back can be the first brave step in a journey worth taking. It's not something I ever could have seen with my six-month-old eyes, but I see it now. As plain as day.

Three-Fold Memories

Grace reveals itself in miniature moments.

One of the most common questions I get from *Little House* fans sounds something like this, "You were only four, how much do you even remember?" It's a logical question with a complex answer that doesn't always satisfy their curiosity. My earliest memories are a mixed bag of confusion. *Do I remember this happening on the set or did I watch it? Or maybe Mom told me the story?*

My sister and I appeared in our first episode at eight-months-old. It's safe to say we have no real memories until Season 8—our last ten months on the set of *Little House on the Prairie*. It's not much to bank on, but those few small memorable moments of being on the show are snapshots cataloged in my brain's Dewey Decimal System.

On the other hand, my mother remembers all sorts of funny scenes and detailed interactions from our years on set. I'm forever grateful for her ability to recall the many experiences we had. She has passed those memories down to me, filling in the blank spots, and supplying me with stories to entertain fans. Another catalogue of memories to rely on. Thanks, Mom.

Maybe the most informative piece of the memory puzzle lies in the show itself. We have a living, breathing account of the four years Brenda and I spent with our television family. Four years of small interactions, miniature moments—with Ma, Pa, and the rest of the cast—all captured on film. As far back as I can remember, watching *Little House on the Prairie* has been part of my life.

Do I have vivid memories of all the stories I tell? Of course not. The Dewey Decimal System has many sources, and I do, too. I rely on three-fold memories: the few memories I have, the stories my mother has told me over the years, and the episodes I have watched. Altogether, they form my multi-layered account of being Baby Grace.

One of the first days on the set, my mom learned a very important lesson: babies on television are just normal babies. They cry when you want them to smile, they get tired and fall asleep, and they soil their diapers at the most inconvenient times. Babies can't be controlled or coached. They don't listen to reason at home or on-screen.

On our first day on set, in the middle of a scene, one of us got fussy. My mom stood off to the side of the camera watching in dismay as Baby Grace cried uncontrollably. She could tell by the look on Mike's face that the shot he envisioned was a no-go. After the scene wrapped, she apologized profusely.

Michael Landon knew the risks of introducing a new addition to the Ingalls family. Babies have the unique ability to disrupt any family, especially a TV family of strangers. He took it as a challenge. Mike reassured her with his gentle smile and experienced composure. "I don't know who Baby Grace is and you don't know who Baby Grace is. Let's let Wendi and Brenda figure it out." He was a brilliant actor and producer, the perfect person to calm the fears of my first-day-on-the-job mom.

In case we didn't know our place in the hierarchy of the cast members, it was spelled out in the shooting schedule of every episode. Each actor was assigned a number. The number would appear at the beginning of every scene the actor was involved in. But not Baby Grace. Baby Grace appeared in the column with all the props and animals.

Two horses.

Cow.

Wheelbarrow.

Baby Grace.

The placement wasn't meant to be demeaning. Baby Grace had no lines to memorize or any integral purpose to accomplish. We didn't even land a contract until Season 7 when Pa couldn't get Baby Grace to eat a thing in the episode "Oleson vs. Oleson." Fans ask if the tears I cried were real, as if a three-year-old knows how to have a fake meltdown. Mike wanted Baby Grace to refuse the breakfast he had prepared and throw a fit, so the crew put a little pepper in my oatmeal. It worked out for the scene and for us beautifully because my "No!" caught on camera transformed us into real actors. Baby Grace moved from extra-pay to a contract with immediate SAG membership. And from then on, our name appeared with all the other actors, our number was six— the sixth member of the Ingalls family.

On workdays, we would leave our house while it was still dark. I can still envision climbing into the backseat of my mom's car, snuggled up with my yellow blanket and sucking my thumb while a stream of headlights lined the highway. It seemed further than twenty-seven miles away, as if we were somehow traveling to the real Walnut Grove. After we parked and walked through the side door of MGM Studios, a long table of pink donut boxes welcomed us to work. We could pick any donut we wanted. It might not seem like a big deal, but to a preschooler life couldn't get any better. It is a memory etched in my brain forever. I still get giddy when I see a pink donut box.

Visitors frequently visited the set, hoping to run into celebrities. An especially overly-animated group of ladies stopped to chat with us with one day. Being so young, we got loads of attention all dressed up in our bonnets and prairie dresses.

One of the ladies crouched down to our level, her eyelids caked with lavender eyeshadow. "Well, aren't you two just the cutest things. Are you actresses?"

At two years old, we hadn't a clue what an actress was, but we did remember what my grandmother always called us: her little movie stars. We even had matching shirts to prove it. Without any hesitation, one of us blurted out. "No, we're movie stars!" The ladies laughed and moved on in search of bigger stars while my mother rolled her eyes with embarrassment.

In the middle of our second season, my parents split up leaving my mom to raise me and my sisters alone. The heavy load of being a single parent was more than she could handle, both practically and financially. *Little House* kept our family afloat, the supportive atmosphere gave my mom community.

On the day we turned three, Brenda and I went to work. Three-year-olds tell everyone when it's their birthday, we weren't any different. The word got around and someone mentioned it to Mike. He knew birthdays were a big deal for kids, so he ordered one of his crew guys to go get us a present.

"Hey boss, what do you want me to get them?"

Mike shrugged his shoulders. "I don't know … how about a big doll?"

To our surprise, two blonde-haired dolls appeared in our dressing room. They were nearly as tall as we were. Delight filled the room, and our hearts swelled to know that "Pa" cared enough to celebrate our birthday. We were thrilled, but I think the gesture meant even more to my mom.

During a typical workday, we spent a lot of time waiting for our turn in front of the camera. We had to be ready at a moment's notice, sitting quietly but just off-screen. The landscape of a soundstage is much smaller than one might imagine. Lights and cameras and cords are scattered about. Actors wait around in high-back director chairs for their scene, then retreat to their dressing rooms for a break.

One day, during a period of prolonged waiting, I climbed into a towering black director's chair trying to occupy my busy toddler-body. Those loose fabric seat panels are not the sturdiest, and I fell out the back causing a ruckus of concern. Within days, new chairs arrived. Bright blue, with our names printed on the backs, and the perfect toddler size. It's one of the only things I still have from the set.

On very special days, we skipped the soundstage and headed to Big Sky Ranch in Simi Valley to shoot the exteriors. After pulling into the dirt parking lot, we climbed aboard a small bus-like vehicle that transported us up and over the curvy one-lane road to Walnut Grove. I'm not sure what got us more excited: the barnyard full of animals, the tree swing, or Bandit's doghouse.

Another highlight was lunchtime—the best hour of the workday at the ranch. The whole cast and crew ate together in a big barn. We loaded our plates high from a long table filled with endless food choices. The chatter around the red-checkered tablecloths, like bees swarming a glass of fresh-squeezed lemonade, is one of my sweetest memories ever.

I'll never forget the Christmas episode of Season 8. Even though the warm California sun blared outside, the joys of Christmas settled over the soundstage. Huge sheets of plastic soared above our heads holding a gazillion tiny tissue-paper-like flecks of snow. The massive fans would begin to blow, someone would holler, "Action", and the magic of falling snowflakes filled the air. We gathered up snowdrifts with our bare hands and even took a box of it home with us.

Months later, we gathered around my grandparent's television set to watch the special holiday episode, the Monday night before Christmas in 1981. I was mesmerized as Baby Grace fell asleep in the rocking chair on Ma's lap, and then in the morning she licked a peppermint stick. When Pa snowshoed from the loft to the barn, Baby Grace cheered at the window with all the kids. It felt like a dream to see myself on television, even though sleeping with Ma wasn't the scene I would have chosen.

There were so many memorable moments: the time spent with Melissa Gilbert (Laura Ingalls) after the tornado episode, my first chance to ride in the back of the wagon with Matt Labyorteaux (Albert Ingalls), hanging out with the other set of twins on the show, Lindsey and Sidney Greenbush (Carrie Ingalls), and the time the crew guys cackled when I stood up to Michael and told him, "No way, José."

All the Baby Grace moments put together don't add up to much screentime. The two-to-three second clips could have been cut and no one would have noticed. The money we made didn't pay for my college tuition or help me become an up-and-coming actor. But what those moments did was create a lasting impression of a family's genuine love for each other. The Ingalls family set the standard of what a loving family looked like. A family I desperately wanted to have at home, but didn't.

Grace reveals itself in miniature moments. It adds up to more than what I could have imagined. To see and document the beauty that unfolded during our years on *Little House* makes my heart swell. One memory at a time.

Throwing Wild Cards

Grace loves in a thousand tiny ways.

Growing up, I spent tons of time at my grandparents' house. Especially during my younger years when my mom needed a well-deserved break from solo parenting. My grandmother, affectionately referred to as Gram, was a meticulously straitlaced lady who could be silly when she felt like it. She didn't give handouts or believe in providing limitless childcare for her grandchildren. On the other hand, Grandpa Gordy didn't have a sharp bone in his body. He wholeheartedly offered to pick Michelle up from preschool and hang out with her until Mom and Brenda and I got home from working on the set.

My grandmother kept an immaculate home, nothing grand but spotless down to the smallest detail. I've never seen carpet so white and the Waterford crystal figurines filled the shelves in perfect array. My sisters and I knew how to behave at Gram's house, and just in case we happened to forget, Mom reminded us every time our car pulled into the driveway.

No running or arguing in the house.

No playing on the stairs.

No touching anything on a shelf.

If you want to be loud or wild, go outside.

My grandpa was nothing like Gram. He horsed around and got in trouble more than we did. If he didn't agree with something she said, he'd start speaking Swedish under his breath. Gram's response was a shocked, "Gord! Not in front of the girls." We had no idea what the words meant but laughed all the same at his mischievous grin. I never saw Grandpa stand up to her, at least not when we were around.

We spent the majority of our time in the family room that led to the backyard, down three mini steps from the main house. It used to be a huge outdoor patio before my grandpa enclosed it and put in a few make-shift door locks on the slider. Long, vertical windows lined all three walls with a built-in upholstered bench running the full length of the longest wall leading out back to the pool house. The other end had a counter with a sink tucked in the far corner and a spare fridge that my grandpa filled with soda pop and chocolate treats. A big round table took up one side of the room, and the rest was open for playing Legos or reading books on the floor where we could stay out of trouble.

My grandparents were good Lutheran people who loved nothing more than Sunday hymns and card games. Besides going to church and swimming in their pool, we played cards at the big round table non-stop. This girl was raised to manage a dozen cards in my small grip by the time I turned six years old.

Grandpa Gordy funded our games of Nickel Down from the depths of his polyester pant pockets. Scrunching his nose, he dug deep to collect the eighty cents we each needed to play the simple variation of Rummy, but with a winner's pot. The moral question of gambling with his elementary age grandchildren didn't even cross his mind. "It's not gambling," he would say, "but a card game with stakes … and life is all about stakes."

During the summer months, when he wasn't giving us turtle

rides on his back across the shallow end of the pool or challenging us to handball against the garage, we played cards with him in the open-air cabana using M&M's instead of nickels. The cabana had a horse-shoe shaped booth, similar to what you'd find in the back corner of a pizza joint.

We'd towel off and climb around the circular seat, our legs sticking to the hot vinyl and water dripping from the ends of our messy blonde hair. The sound of the Dodgers game blared from an old black-and-white television set in the background, a metal antenna arranged just so. Depending on the weather and how long the baseball game went, Grandpa had a spare bowl of M&M's sitting in the fridge in case our first round of chocolate "nickels" started melting. His life seemed to revolve around us kids.

Whenever we played cards, my sisters and I begged to sit next to Grandpa. We drew straws or rolled dice to determine who got the golden seat next to his. Being on his left side meant receiving the mishandled wild cards that would magically appear on top of the deck. He'd peek into the lucky seat-holder's hand and throw the one card she needed to win the round, and a bowlful of nickels. He tried to play the fool but not successfully, his smirk gave it away every time. My card-shark grandmother did not appreciate his generosity, but we sure did.

After he visited our house, we might find one crisp Washington dollar under each of our pillows or maybe a stack of quarters beside our toothbrushes. Sometimes he'd leave a check in my parent's desk drawer for them to discover later or hide a hundred-dollar bill in the toilet paper roll of the master bathroom. Whimsical, full of unexpected surprises, that's how he demonstrated love.

He used to polish the slides at the park with Pledge furniture spray, play tic-tac-toe on the back of the bulletin during church services, and take us to the most magical places. It wasn't the size of the gift that made such an impression on me, but the love he displayed wherever he went. Never a harsh word, he exhaled love and compassion.

Grandpa Gordy was a gift giver—the most unselfish person I've ever known. His biggest thrill came at watching us succeed, surprising us with silly acts of kindness usually involving money or sweet treats or trips to see and do things that would leave us wide-eyed and giggling. He cared more about us than winning a game or an argument with my grandmother.

Grandpa's gifts were like those wild cards in Nickel Down: unexpected and undeserved, but always leaving us with a giddy hope that he would do something—anything. For we never knew what that something might be and to be honest, we didn't really care. It came from the goodness of his heart. A heart of gold.

Back in 1993, my grandpa received a terminal diagnosis of leukemia. He only had a few weeks to live, and we spent one last Easter with him at my grandparents' house. He did his best not to show how sick he was, but his pale sunken cheeks hung over his jawbone. His once sparkling blue eyes appeared life-less and spent, abandoned robin's eggs that would never hatch. Regardless, Grandpa Gordy put on his polyester pants as usual, his pockets full of spare change, and a soft smile resting on his too-frail face.

I'll never forget our last game of Nickel Down. There were twelve of us at the table, all scrunched in so we could fit. Grandpa sighed heavy, we could tell he needed to rest, but he pulled out eighty cents for each of us grandkids—our last grand-pa-funded game. One of us sat next to him—I can't remember who, but it wasn't me. He snickered and peeked like always, threw the last wild cards of his life and then the game was over. Grandpa would soon be gone. His love, a memory in our hearts.

His life, a wet canvas of color illustrating mankind's ability to love in much the same way as God. Wildly unexpected, free of charge and free of judgment.

He spoke with his oldest sister just days before he went home to Jesus. She recalled the conversation as nothing short of a miraculous perspective, a grace-filled embrace of his end coming earlier than we all expected. Grandpa focused on the many blessings he'd experienced over his lifetime and how his very full life wasn't over, not yet. He would live on through his children and grandchildren.

That spring of my sophomore year of high school is a blur even now. I had never experienced death before, the unexpected nature of it clocked me over the head. It broke my heart to lose my Grandpa Gordy, the first man I could depend on to never leave me. To always love me, with no strings attached.

My grandpa knew all about getting something he never expected. His lifetime of memories easily could have never happened for him. As a young man, he served as an aerial photographer in the U.S. Airforce during World War II. He joined the "Half-A-Hundred Club" for completing his 50th combat mission on a B-24 bomber. I remember when he showed us his scrapbook one afternoon, the thick black pages held picture after picture of his friends in their uniforms, standing next to their planes, smiling and hugging each other.

There was one especially memorable photo of a young pilot sitting inside a huge hole in the side of his plane—the metal peeled back like petals of a flower. His pilot friend held his hands together in the prayer posture and looked up to the sky, as if to say, "Thank you, Lord, for letting me make it back." Grandpa told us that he was one of the lucky few who came home from the war. Some of his buddies never made it back, they didn't have the chance to get married, have children, or slip wild cards to their grandchildren.

For my grandpa, living another day was grace. Getting the chance to be love to the little people in his life gave him immeasurable joy. I think he learned how to love from God himself. Over the top, whimsical, wild, and free.

Grace loves in a thousand tiny ways. Whether it be a bird showing up out of nowhere or chocolate candies melting in a bowl. Love is as exciting as a wild card staring you in the face and longing to be picked up, hitting the jackpot of nickels, and then realizing the real jackpot is sitting right next to you.

A Family Affair

Grace welcomes outsiders into a family.

We don't all come from naturally happy families. While my *Little House* family was more than ideal, my parents' tumultuous marriage didn't last long. I don't remember much, but I do remember a babysitter putting us to bed in our small apartment while my mom worked nights as a waitress. I know my mom longed for a different story, a story of happily-ever-after. Not just for her sake, but for us girls too. It was the beginning of a search—a search for someone who loved us enough to stick around and lead our family. We needed a captain to command our crew of lost and wandering girls.

During our last season of *Little House*, my mom married my stepdad, Lanny. We won him over with our giggles and towhead blonde hair. He won us over with his goofy smile and steady nature. A gentle, loyal man shoved into a basketball player's body—long and lanky—with a contagious laugh as entertaining as any joke. He used to tease that most grooms went home with a wife after the wedding, but he left the reception with a family of five. We never called him our stepdad, he was "Daddy" to me and my sisters from Day One.

After a quick weekend honeymoon, we moved in with him. The house had three big bedrooms and even a bathroom for me and my sisters to call our own. The floorplan created a circle, with lots of doors connecting the rooms to each other. Perfect for a game of tag, but also perfect because the bond of love could grow there.

Out the sliding glass door, a huge grass lawn welcomed us with a low concrete wall on one side stepping up like stairs every so often. The short part of the wall acted as our balance beam and as our courage rose, so did the wall. It traveled back to meet a steep hill of ice plants spanning the entire length of the backyard with bright pink and yellow flowers dotting the landscape. I'd never seen so many flowers in one place. Our previous apartment didn't have a yard and we weren't allowed to pick flowers at the park even if we found one. Our new backyard was a dream come true.

Not long after we moved in, my stepdad designed and built a playhouse for us. This was no ordinary tree fort. The little boxed-in room had windows and a pitched roof with a connecting deck that soared higher than the roof of our house—the perfect place to camp out with sleeping bags and watch the stars. The ladder descended to an open-air kitchen, with a sink that drained, and we'd haul water with a bucket from the spout on the side yard. The love and creativity flowing from that man's hands blew me away. More extravagant than I thought possible, considering he barely knew us. It didn't take long for us to bond as a family.

Most weekends during the summer and fall we packed up my stepdad's Chevy van and headed to the lake. My dad and a few of his friends shared a boat, which waited for us at the end of a long, very splintery dock. Sometimes the boat started right up, other times it sputtered and quit, meaning the engine needed some work. It didn't bother us one bit, jumping off the dock into the water and visiting the marina's roll top icebox for cold treats kept us more than happy. My stepdad came alive at the lake, more than any other place on the planet. I think God created him to forever wear swim trunks, in search of glassy coves and sandy beaches for us to enjoy.

When the cold weather kept us away from the lake, we spent time with my newly acquired grandparents. They had four kids, including my dad, and all of them were married. Overnight, I had a whole new family, aunts and uncles and cousins galore. My Grandma Bonnie was as sweet as the sugar squares that filled the china bowl on the counter, which I know because Uncle Kevin used to sneak one for me and each of my sisters when no one was looking.

One Saturday, over deviled eggs and Jell-O layered salad, the family came together to start a project in my grandparents' front yard. It involved all of us, but the men did most of the work. We spent long weekends and countless weeknights with tape measures and raspy saws that left behind little piles of sawdust.

First, they built two long rectangular-shaped hollow boxes out of wood, not much wider than I was tall, spanning about thirty feet. The air bit our throats as they coated the boxes with layers of fiberglass and arranged them side-by-side with a six-foot gap between the two. The focus then shifted to the floor and framing up the walls.

Pretty soon a structure resembling a long, narrow house began to take shape. It must have been about the size of our old apartment, but not at all like a normal house. The corners of the floor sat on the smelly fiberglass boxes along the outer edges, creating a tunnel down the middle, under the floor. We could have crawled on our hands and knees all the way through if only Grandpa Daryl would have let us.

The front deck had a sliding glass door that led to a room with a counter and the tiniest stove I'd ever seen. Across the way, a mini fridge sat at an angle in the corner with a radio positioned just above. Taking a few steps farther, we came to a set of bunk beds directly across from a small bathroom, so small that my stepdad had to duck to get through the opening. A compact sink and a toilet with a foot flusher were hidden behind a door that disappeared inside the wall and locked with the turn of a little brass lever.

The back room had a closet and a wooden platform with a cushion that folded out to make a bed. A door led to the back deck with a hatch on the floor that opened with the pull of a flat silver knob to reveal a big empty compartment. My stepdad called it the engine room. Apparently, this thing could drive on water.

My grandpa made a wooden sign in his shop and hung it across from the kitchen sink where I was told the table would be. I didn't know what "A Family Affair" meant but it must have been important because they painted it on the exterior too, right outside a little window next to the steering wheel with a set of gauges like a car.

On the wall to the left of the steering wheel, above the throttle, was a golden bell. My dad told us to never ring the bell, only the captain could use it to alert the crew. He rang it with intensity.

"All hands on deck." He yelled as if he had turned pirate. "Looks like I've got three volunteer crew members right here."

Our eyes widened, looking at each other and not thinking it could be true.

We were part of the crew—part of a family.

I had found my captain.

I could hardly believe that Lanny was ours. A dad who came home for dinner every single night. He made his share of parenting blunders, but ultimately, he stepped into the role of fathering us three girls with such grace. In him, we'd found a gold mine in every way.

After the family completed building the houseboat, my grandparents retired to a little town with a huge lake about seven hours north of us. They lived in a real house a short drive away, but the floating house became a second home to them—to all of us. Every summer from then on, we waited for our turn on the lake. We loaded the van down heavy with sleeping bags and blue Igloo coolers, enough bacon and eggs and marshmallows to last us two weeks, and the ski-boat on its trailer followed closely behind.

Over the years, my dad taught me a lot. He showed me how to drive the houseboat and how to scout for rocks when pulling into a sandy beach. I learned to secure the long ropes around big boulders or tree trunks along the shore with special sailing knots, and how to give those ropes some slack as the water levels dropped. I knew how to mop the decks and store the cargo for the next voyage. My dad taught me the ins and outs of working on a crew, but he took responsibility for everything. If I messed up, he just showed me again.

There's nothing better than being part of a crew—a family where love and respect are upheld. Every crew has a captain, and the crew follows the captain anywhere. Lanny didn't demand our love and respect right away. He knew it would take time. When I joined my stepdad's crew, my life changed drastically. I was dearly loved and accepted without having to prove myself worthy. I didn't do anything to earn his love, but joyfully embraced it. Honoring him came easy.

I didn't know then what I do know now. My stepdad modeled a version of love I'd never experienced. Lanny loved and cared for children who were not his own. He paved the way for the greatest Captain of all time to offer me a place on His crew. My stepdad showed me how.

I've heard little girls being referred to as their daddy's "little princess." It wasn't a nickname I ever received or even wanted. Being a princess has never intrigued me but being a *daughter* does. Having a Daddy, that speaks straight to my heart.

I've always believed that love is stronger than blood, much stronger than legal documents. My stepdad proved it. He loved three little girls who belonged to someone else on paper, but more than made up for it with his unending love. No judge in a courtroom had the power to take that truth away. It was an adoption of the heart.

Someone once asked me about the name of our houseboat, *A Family Affair* could be taken several ways. I always thought it implied a secret place reserved for family to gather together. A place of rest and relaxation, away from the pressures of the world. Maybe it's what my grandparents intended to convey—our little slice of heaven here on earth.

For me, our beloved houseboat was where I learned to be a crew member of the most caring man I've ever known.

From Acting to Kindergarten

Grace knows when to call it quits.

I looked down at a tan fringed vest, my just-a-hair-too-big matching cowboy hat had slipped down over my eyes. I pulled the lanyard tight against my chin and tilted the brim far enough up to see the holster strapped around my waist. *This is the coolest outfit ever*, I thought. *I don't ever want to take it off.*

With my arm extended to the sky, the plastic white-butted pistol was cocked and ready. I smiled the biggest smile I ever remember smiling for a camera, standing next to a set of twin boys with phony bows and arrows, each of them decked out in a feather headdress. Brenda and I were having the day of our lives—our first appearance in a commercial.

Our role as Baby Grace ended in the spring of 1982 when the Ingalls family moved away from Walnut Grove in the last episode of Season 8. Around the same time, my mom married my step-dad, Lanny. It was a turning point for our family in more ways than one. We exchanged a TV family for a real family and then my parents had to decide whether Brenda and I would continue our acting careers. The decision dragged on for more than a year after *Little House* ended.

The next season of the series would be centered on Laura and

Almanzo, and their little girl, Rose. With Baby Grace no longer needed, our agent went to work, determined to get us our next gig, and soon. My mom reluctantly went along with it, not knowing what to expect.

Our initial audition for McDonald's didn't go too well. The first indication materialized when the producer showed Brenda and me a photo in our preliminary interview. To us, Ronald McDonald was a scary red-haired clown dressed up in yellow overalls. We had no idea who he was or what a Happy Meal even tasted like.

On the ride home, my mom wanted to know how it went. "So, what did the producer ask you girls?"

Brenda piped up from the backseat. "Nothing much. He showed us a picture of a crazy-looking man with red curly hair and lipstick. Then asked if we liked McDonald's french fries."

"Have we ever had McDonald's french fries, Mom?" I asked with a confused look on my face.

It's no wonder why we didn't receive a callback. As preschoolers, who were accustomed to the favored treatment on the set of *Little House*, we assumed we must have done something wrong to not get the part. My mom recalls one of us asking why they didn't like us after our agent called with the disappointing news. She tried to defuse the moment, explaining that maybe the producer was looking for dark-haired twins. In the back of her mind, she began to realize that the life of a child actor would involve a healthy dose of rejection.

Strike one, but our agent didn't give up.

Child actors require a parent or guardian to cart them from place to place for all sorts of interviews, a tedious job. By the time our next audition came around my mom was pregnant with my little sister, Heidi. She wanted to give our acting careers a fair chance but also didn't know realistically how long it could go on.

There was a first audition with a producer, then a callback with a panel of bigwigs. After our agent called and told my mom we got the role, she sent us for yet another outing to meet with the wardrobe director to get fitted for our western getups. The one-day shoot turned out to be a drawn-out exhausting day for my pregnant mom. I remember the outfits and the excitement, but Mom remembers a whole other scenario.

University Bank of Texas had hired us and the other set of twins to promote their new telephone banking feature. The frazzled mom held a phone up to her ear while Cowgirl Brenda shot her play pistols at the feathered headdress circling the kitchen island. The chanting of the little blonde boy made it impossible to hear the menu of options from the automated teller.

After more takes than Mom could count, Brenda finally got a break. The advertisement spiel highlighted the conveniences of banking in the luxury of your own home. No need to load those crazy kids into the car. The only challenge might be how to keep them quiet. That's where my scene came in as the camera panned from the kitchen to a set of chairs, the other little boy twin and I tied back-to-back, each with a lollipop in our mouths.

There are all sorts of problems with the content of this commercial, but in the early 80s my mom's only concern rested on what would be best for us girls and her growing family. The family-like atmosphere on *Little House on the Prairie* stood head-and-shoulders over a normal film crew. The sheer number of kids running around the prairie for nine seasons transformed the typical work environment on a soundstage to accommodate child-labor laws, schoolwork to be completed, and a place for child actors to thrive. At least half of the cast still attended school and their parents wanted them home in time for dinner. Working commercials was more than a step down from *Little House*.

On a one-day commercial shoot, the producers didn't know

our names. There was no relationship to build, nor much concern if the five-year-old twins were tired or hungry. My mom noticed the difference immediately and by the time we drove home she knew our first commercial would be our last.

She called up our agent and said goodbye.

When fans ask why I didn't continue my acting career, I tell them. "We graduated from acting and went to Kindergarten." It was a simple decision for my mother. She wanted to give us and my sisters a normal childhood, a life similar to what the Ingalls family depicted on-screen. No lights or cameras, no learning lines or auditions with producers. No rejections. Just a good, old-fashioned family living life together.

My mom had the wisdom to walk away from the Hollywood scene. To realize that even the greatest experiences come to an end. She had the grace to know when to call it quits. And for that I am forever grateful.

Soaring Kites & Twirly Skirts
Grace values individual strengths.

I grew up with an identical twin sister, it's all I ever knew. Mirror twins have matching faces and sound the same, but they are different too. Brenda is right-handed and I'm a lefty. My sister instinctively paved a path for me to follow. The first-born, first to sit up and crawl and walk, first to hold a crayon and scribble on the back of the Baby Grace photos we would autograph for fans. She led the way, and I followed her around like a lost puppy looking for a friend.

Everyone mixed us up. That's the plight of being a twin. It was a perpetual name explanation everywhere we went. Even my mom struggled to tell us apart at times. As newborns, she noticed a dark vein across my right eyelid, it became the secret clue to determine who was who.

As Brenda and I got older, our personalities became more pronounced. People started to notice the differences, especially our teachers. Brenda worked hard and knew what she wanted, she did whatever it took to attain it. I had my head in the clouds most of the time.

One day during a parent-teacher conference, my mom discovered just how distinct our temperaments could be. Mom settled herself into a miniature chair on the round side of the half-circle activity table. My first-grade teacher, Mrs. Draeger, sat across from her with two file folders and two oversized pieces of off-white paper.

"Wendi and Brenda are doing fine academically. They are engaged in class and get along with the other students. I wanted to show you a recent art assignment. The way they look at the world couldn't be more different."

Mrs. Draeger slid the pages across the moon-shaped table, waiting for my mother to respond. Not a word was heard as she focused her attention to the first drawing featuring a solid gray almost-straight rectangle standing tall on a street. Evenly spaced rows of small squares filled the structure, arranged as perfectly as a waxy crayon could manage. Brenda had scrawled, "A building is high," above the drawing and penned her name with perfection in the bottom right corner of the page. Remarkable.

My mom set the first drawing aside and smiled at the explosion of color on the next sheet of paper. A single squiggly string attached to a colorful diamond-shaped object soared in a bright blue sky. It illustrated my printed description, "A kite is high." The tail of the aircraft blew sideways, a long ribbon with an oversized bow. The different images and colors surprised both my teacher and my mom. How could twins be so much alike and yet so different?

"The word 'high' was the drawing prompt. I couldn't help but notice how their personalities are accentuated through their artwork. Their strengths shine." Mrs. Draeger's warm smile met my mother's eyes.

"Yes, I see it too. How fascinating. I think I'm going to have my hands full with these two." My mom chuckled and tucked the drawings under her arm as she left the classroom. The conversation resurfaced later when she came home. From then on, she called me her little kite.

My six-year-old carefree spirit embraced the nickname with

every bit of my heart. I loved to soar all over the place, but I also loved the security of being a twin. Most days, we dressed alike, and every day was an endless sleepover with my best friend.

My mom never believed in creating an easy path for her children, instead she let life unfold naturally for us. Growing up has its challenges, throw being a twin into the equation and it's likely to get a little messy: friend troubles, competition over grades and sports, attempting to establish an identity apart from each other. Being a twin proved to be much harder than I ever thought it would be. The constant comparison started internally for me and grew with each passing year. By the time third grade rolled around, I was struggling in a big way.

One school-day morning, my mom walked down the hall to our bedroom. Michelle, Brenda, and I shared one room, and my little sister Heidi was in the nursery. A soft rap on the door jerked my eyes open.

"Time to get moving. Cinnamon toast will be ready in ten minutes."

I laid there, staring at the ceiling while concocting a strategy. *The living room. Yes, it's the perfect plan.* Quietly, I snuck out of bed, pulling my comforter up as flat as possible, my pillow fluffed and centered. I wanted my sisters to think I got up early. My bare feet poked out of my ankle-length nightgown, not at all ready for school. *Mom's not going to be happy if she sees me.* I sprinted into the empty living room, then pretended to search for something by the sofa to buy myself some time. My eyes peered around the corner into the kitchen, trying to see if my sisters had arrived. I didn't want to attract too much attention, or my mother standing at the counter buttering cinnamon toast would shoo me back to my room to get dressed. Then my plan would be ruined.

My older sister, Michelle, came around the corner. She looked over at me with raised eyebrows, as if to kindly reprimand my actions. Michelle had always been a bit of a mother hen to us, but she didn't say a word as she perched next to my mom who was stacking the toast high on a single plate. Mom carried it to the middle of the kitchen table and started loading the dishwasher.

Brenda strode into the room. I eyed her from head to toe. I saw confidence radiating from her, a vision of perfection to my young eyes. I didn't have her determination or the pinpoint focus that kept her grounded and working towards a goal. She had a drive to succeed, steered by pure courage and tenacity. I wanted what she had more than anything and reasoned that maybe her confident spirit would rub off on me.

A split second later, I raced back to my closet, replaying the mental picture in my mind… jeans, my blue tee, and sneakers. Nothing fancy but I was ready.

I hurried back to the kitchen and sat down in my chair, sinking my teeth into a piece of sugary cinnamon toast. My eyes stayed down, and I bit my lip in anxiety-filled anticipation. A heavy sigh came from across the wooden table. Brenda huffed in aggravation, slamming her empty plate in front of her. Bits of sugar went flying.

"Mom! She's dressed like me again. Make her change."

The tears slowly pooled then trickled down my cheeks. I didn't understand.

What's so wrong with dressing alike?

The scene had played out this way before. Some mornings my mom led me down the hall to our shared closet to find another outfit. Me blubbering the entire way. Other mornings, Brenda got up without a word and disappeared into the bedroom to do it herself. It wasn't that she didn't like being a twin, but she longed for independence and an identity of her own. I craved belonging and affirmation. In my mind, dressing alike provided a sense of safety.

One Saturday morning not long after the blue-shirt-and-jeans incident, I began to grasp the importance of individual strengths—how my uniqueness could be celebrated. Mom had been racking her brain, trying to solve the dilemma of morning tears and fights over matching outfits. A seamstress by necessity and trade, she naturally found the answer with one stop at the fabric store. Surrounded by bolts of colorful fabric, I had an enormous choice to make.

"You think you can find some fabric for a twirly skirt? I'm making it just for you."

Just for me? My eyes swelled with excitement at the thought of a new circle skirt—the ultimate eight-year-old outfit. I don't think I understood what those words meant. Twins generally share everything, especially clothes—at least we did.

I paced round and round the carousels of printed cotton. Pinks and yellows and blues, how could I ever pick? The choices overwhelmed me, but I didn't want to miss my chance at a new twirly skirt. And then I saw it, a deep red fabric with zoo animals printed in black.

I'd never seen anything like it. Nor had Mom, chuckling, as I ran over to her at the cutting counter with the bolt of fabric in my arms. My mom smiled as I proudly presented it to the lady with the scissors.

"You are my one and only Wendi. No one could pull it off but you."

For a moment, I wondered what Brenda would think. *Would she want one too? Would she ask to borrow it?* Then my mother's words repeated themselves in my mind and I realized that some things don't come in pairs. I didn't need to dress like Brenda. It was a hard slow lesson of learning to love the person I was made to be.

Thanks to an elastic waistband, I lived in that skirt for nearly two years. It represented the first small step in grasping what it meant to be fearfully and wonderfully made. I was created wonderfully different than my sister. We each had our own set of individual strengths. The shift of thinking changed everything for me, God's words delivered through my mother's voice. Moms are like that, dishing out wisdom completely unaware at times. *I could be extraordinary all by myself.*

God uses wise people, and sometimes twirly skirts, to reveal how much He loves His creation. Thank goodness for moms—especially moms who sew—but also for teachers and mentors who have helped me find myself along the way.

I'm still a fan of skirts that twirl. There's something about them that makes me happy inside. My mom has made more than a few twirly skirts for me over my lifetime, but one has been hanging in my closet for over twenty-five years. It's the ultimate twirler, crafted from colorful neckties with a hem of diamond-shaped points.

Every once in a while, I bust it out and twirl, just for the fun of it. Just to remember how much God loves the one-of-a-kind creation he's made. And in the back of my mind, I hear my mother's voice and smile. *No one can pull it off but you.*

The Six Weeks
That Lasted Forever

Grace endures the wait.

A lady in a black pantsuit scrolled the dial of circular numbers on the square metal box hanging from the doorknob. As the correct combination aligned, the little compartment opened revealing a key. My sisters and I peered through the obscured inset of glass as she unlocked the deadbolt. We flooded in, all six of us, to explore the last of the three houses on the market in our price range.

My parents had one weekend to find a place to live before returning to Southern California to pack and move four hours north to the little town of Atascadero. School would be starting in a few months, and the excitement in our eyes was hardly containable.

The small landing of the entryway stepped up to a living room with just enough space for our couch, wicker loveseat, and the entertainment center back home. Moving into the kitchen, my mom switched on the overhead lightbox and peered into the cupboards. My footsteps clicked against the off-white linoleum floor. The squares of powder blue flowers led to a back slider and a deck overlooking a patch of overgrown grass.

"This house feels like us. Doesn't it?" My sister Michelle said what we were all thinking. "Except, maybe the backyard."

"In time, we can work on the yard. That won't be a problem. You girls want to check out the bedrooms?" My dad led the way down the hallway, the four of us girls close on his heels.

Brenda and I barreled through the first door. An average-sized room with a huge closet, it checked off all the necessary boxes. *A little decorating and I'd be more than happy.* "Looks good to me."

She nodded in agreement as we entered the second bedroom.

My older sister, Michelle, held little Heidi's hand as she crouched down eye to eye with our three-year-old sister. "Your bed could go right here, and mine will be on the far wall. We're going to have so much fun together."

Heidi beamed with delight. She had never shared a room with the big girls before. She hugged Michelle and wouldn't let go.

My parents emerged from the master bedroom, a bit bigger than the others, with a small ensuite bath on the other side of the closet.

My dad nodded approvingly. "Every man needs the privacy of a second bathroom, especially in a house with five girls."

We all giggled and filed out of the front door, every one of us, giddy and convinced it would be our new home. My parents signed a stack of papers, the sellers accepted the offer, and we went home to start packing. We spent the summer waiting for escrow to close, dreaming of our new house.

Weeks turned into months, and September crept closer and closer. The thought of starting the fourth grade at a new school was like having dessert on a school night. Moving into a new house would be a cherry on top.

The weekend before school started, we packed everything from the old house into a big moving truck. Escrow hadn't closed, so it all went into a storage unit.

The realtor said, "A week, tops."

Our van pulled into the Motel 6 parking lot. My heart sank. Duffle bags slung over our shoulders, we ascended the exterior metal stairwell, my dad holding a green oval keychain with our room number engraved into the plastic. Ignoring a rowdy group of adults gathered around the outdated motel pool, he twisted the key in the lock. The door swung open to reveal two double beds and a bathroom the size of a linen closet.

Dropping her bag in the doorway, Brenda ran across the room and jumped onto the bed. "This one's ours!"

My dad smirked with a sideways grin. "It'll be yours half of the time, the other half you'll be camping out on the floor with one of your sisters."

"What about Charlie?" Brenda replied with concern over our black cocker spaniel.

My dad exhaled a mouthful of air and rolled his eyes. "Don't worry, we'll make room for Charlie too."

Six people and a dog in one motel room required some real organization. Our four small duffle bags and my parent's suitcase crowded the far side of the platform holding the television. We lined up our sneakers and backpacks near the door. The old brown cooler fit right under the bathroom sink, doubling as a counter for my mom to pack our sack lunches.

Breakfast took place at the park across the street. With four squirrely girls and no place to eat besides the beds, it made the most sense. On cereal mornings, my mom unloaded a stack of shallow paper bowls and a pack of white plastic spoons onto the wood picnic table, along with a quart of milk and a box of cereal. We ate until the cereal was gone. If any milk remained after we'd had our fill, it had to be thrown out. We learned the hard way that an opened milk container couldn't survive in the cooler overnight.

Most evenings, we went to Bob's Big Boy where my dad ordered a "home-cooked" meal. We climbed around the circular booth in the corner, all scrunched in and hungry. My mom knew how to stretch a dollar, and she showed off her improvising skills with ease.

"Can we get the Deluxe Burger with fries and four small plates for the girls? I'll split it up for them... and then I'd like the all-you-can-eat salad bar, please."

After the food came, my mom cut the burger in fourths, split up the fries, and transferred a small portion of veggies from her salad onto each of our plates. And every once in a while, she ordered a hot fudge sundae for dessert—one sundae with six spoons.

Every time the hotel phone rang, we held our breath hoping for good news. Hoping that the wait would soon be over. Two weeks turned into four. Before we knew it, the summer changed to fall, mornings at the park grew colder, and we were talking about Halloween costumes. I never imagined the wait would be so long.

It wasn't all bad: the motel pool cut down on our shower time, the tables at McDonald's gave us a flat surface to do homework on, and we found a way to get along in very close quarters. We learned to give each other grace and to be thankful for even the smallest sense of privacy—especially my dad.

Escrow finally closed in the middle of October. We worked together and unloaded every box with gratefulness in our hearts. The road God paved for us to relocate to Atascadero started off pretty rough, but it led to a wonderful future. Our new home was worth the wait.

Of all the many lessons God has taught over my lifetime, I

think the most difficult seasons have been the waiting seasons. The times when my hands are tied and there's nothing left for me to do but simply wait. Hours turn into days and days melt into weeks. The wait feels as though it will never end.

In those periods of time, when my mind is antsy and impatient, I come to a crossroad, a point of desperation. I can't take another step forward. My lungs won't breathe another breath. The only alternative is surrender. Releasing the illusion of control has been a serious challenge for me. At times, it felt like being placed in a prescribed time-out. I could kick and scream all I wanted, but a tantrum never solves the problem. Grace endures the wait no matter how long it goes on.

Patience doesn't come naturally for me. It is a slowly built virtue formed over lengthy periods of waiting. I have a long way to go, but there's nothing like the fullness of a thankful heart after the wait is over. Living in a motel for six weeks was my first real waiting season, an opportunity to develop patience at a young age. My family learned how to surrender every day to the One who knew exactly when our house would be ready. The wait was long, but God had a purpose.

I've spent a lot of time waiting. Waiting in traffic. Waiting for test results. Waiting for prayers to be answered and waiting for escrows to close. Whether it's six minutes, six weeks, or even longer, there is a purpose in the waiting. And I don't want to miss it.

Seventy Times Seven

Grace forgives because He's forgiven us.

The packed chapel pews brimmed with high school students sitting shoulder to shoulder. Not more than a foot of space to call my own. A steady stream of cool mountain air blew through the opened side doors, the sound of chirping crickets making its way to my ears. As the lights went low and the band slowed its melody, I let the familiar words pass without a second thought.

All had sinned. Check.
Jesus died for our transgressions. Check.
The gift of God is eternal life through Jesus. Check.
Confess with your mouth, believe in your heart. Check.
There is now no condemnation for those in Christ Jesus. Amen.

And then our camp speaker said something my fourteen-year-old ears had never considered before: "If God forgives our mistakes, why don't we forgive others?" He said that unforgiveness inside our hearts puts a wall between us and God. I hadn't ever considered it. His next remark grabbed my attention, "For some of you, it's time to tear the wall down."

I'd heard an altar call plenty of times before. I was raised in the church. I sang in kid's choir and volunteered in the nursery every Sunday night after my twelfth birthday. I felt as though God and I had a good thing going. My faith was on cruise control until those words stabbed me in the heart. *Forgive? How could I forgive him?*

The gospel message I heard that night urged a roomful of teenagers to take one step farther. It required something from me—not just knowing in my head but letting it trickle down into my heart. Changing the way I lived. The challenge was to backup what I said I believed. Put feet on faith, to do the very thing Jesus had done for me.

It wouldn't be easy, unforgiveness ran deep through my bones. I had been carrying it for as long as I could remember. Facing my bitterness head-on in the chapel forced me to unearth my critical mindset, one I'd long ago identified as acceptable. Harboring resentment never seemed like a big deal before. I couldn't ignore it any longer.

Long story short: my biological father walked out on us, leaving my mom to care for and support three preschool-aged girls alone. His involvement was minimal until my mom remarried a few years later. Then he reinserted himself into our world, demanding his paternal rights. The judge awarded my father biweekly visits. Thank goodness, I had my sisters to keep me company.

Weekends at his home were forced. I never wanted to go. His raised voice brought me to tears. His crew of rough friends made me uncomfortable. I cried and begged my mom to let us stay home. The court ruling had her hands tied.

After our move to Atascadero, my father made one last trip

to see us. Michelle had just celebrated a birthday, so he wanted to take her out for a fancy dinner. I knew my mom was worried when she tucked two dimes in Michelle's shoe and gave her a quick lesson on how to call from a pay phone. Relief swept over us when his car pulled into the driveway a few hours later with Michelle safely at home.

The awkward exchange of half-hearted hugs on the front lawn closed that chapter of my life. I never saw my father again, and yet, he wouldn't allow my stepdad to adopt us girls either. A deep-rooted resentment grew in my heart. I justified my feelings, declaring them as well-deserved. I moved on and never imagined changing the way I felt about him.

Until the night when the camp speaker paced the stage. He stopped and looked right at me. I felt his blue eyes begging me to let go of the bitterness that pulsed in my heart. I didn't want to let go of my resentment, it felt right to judge him. *Didn't my father deserve it?*

Our speaker paused and pulled out a calculator from the back pocket of his jeans. He placed it on the overhead projector and punched in a series of numbers.

70 X 7 = 490

When Jesus told Peter to forgive his brother seventy times seven from the gospel of Matthew, He wasn't giving Peter permission to keep track. Quite the opposite. I had been keeping a running total of my father's shortcomings all my life. In fact, I relished keeping track.

The speaker challenged us, "How many offenses will it take before you stop adding them up? Jesus doesn't keep a tally of our offenses. Will you ever stop counting?"

The truth of the pastor's words landed heavy in the room. Not a whisper. We were invited to stay or leave respectfully. As my friends shuffled down the long pews and out the door to a huge sky of stars surrounded by pine trees, my conflicted spirit cemented my feet to the chapel floor.

I knew what had to be done. Not for my father's sake, but for mine. To move on and let the bitterness die. If I wanted to receive the gift of forgiveness, then my days of counting the transgressions of my father needed to be over. All the nights we spent alone, every harsh and careless word he'd spoken, the long list of broken promises, the all-out brawls with my mom, the selfish pride that kept him from signing adoption papers. Every infraction. Every outburst. Every moment of my childhood that felt wrong needed to be surrendered. I'd never realized the satisfaction it gave me until that moment. I repeated the words again in my head. *When will you ever stop counting?*

I sat in the pew, my elbows propped on my knees, my ponytail covering my wet cheeks. I didn't know how it would all work out, but I had to try. I wanted to let go of the anger and the hurt inside. My camp counselor showed me how.

As I sat in the chapel, I learned that forgiveness doesn't forget what happened, but it does choose to pardon the offender. It chooses to recognize that people are sometimes limited in their life experience, and they don't always have the ability to fulfill the role they've been given to complete. I like to think my father did the best he could. Perhaps his parenting skills lacked wisdom because of the family he grew up in. Sadly, he missed out on having a relationship with his three daughters.

After reframing the reasoning behind my father's actions, I didn't have to be angry anymore. I could begin to forgive him. Even when it felt impossible. Even when he didn't do anything to earn my forgiveness. I could willingly give it to him. A gift of grace with no strings attached.

It's funny because I want that kind of grace, too. And what you freely give away tends to come back.

Never Forgotten

Grace sees us, even when others do not.

The half-time buzzer rang. Five players with their bouncing ponytails charged off the court, headed straight for the orange water jug. The tall stack of Dixies sat on a rolling cart at the end of a row of metal chairs.

Those of us on the bench stood and gathered around the outer edge of the huddle, giving the starters our seats to rest their tired legs. My twin sister, Brenda, was right in the middle of the bench, chattering about the opposing star forward and her hard screens. One high-five turned into ten, contagiously traveling around the circle of freshmen and sophomores.

The energy in the gym dissipated as our coach squatted in front of the bench, scribbling XX's on a whiteboard. "Great defense out there, ladies." His flushed face barked out the second-half strategy, "Watch number twenty-one, get a hand in her face so she can't take a shot. Full-court press after every bucket. We aren't letting this lead slip from our hands." We nodded our heads in agreement.

He rose to his feet just as the lighted numbers ran down to zero and the horn blew to signal the resume of play. I held my breath, hoping Coach would let me start the second half, but he didn't call my name before the team cheered, "Greyhounds!" Freshmen weren't guaranteed playing time, but my heart sank as I watched Brenda disappear from the bench and check in at the score table. Again.

The stalky referee bounced the leather basketball from the center of the court, a whistle dangling from his mouth. Looking up to the scoreboard, I beamed with pride at the twelve-point lead my team had created. A big enough lead to give everyone some playing time, I hoped. *Surely Coach will put you in. Just be patient, Wendi.*

Our team dominated the next twelve minutes, the hefty lead only grew larger by the time the buzzer rang to begin the fourth quarter. No question about it, this game was in the bag. But there I sat feeling pretty lousy about myself. *What's the deal? I've been to every practice all season... same as Brenda.*

Everyone on the bench had been in several times, sweat dripping from their earlobes and their arms shiny and wet. My teammates grinned, fully lost in the success of the moment. I pretended to be fine, as if being invisible didn't bother me. But just under the surface, a deep sadness grew. I wanted to walk out of there, or at least douse my quivering throat with some water. No luck, the stack of miniature paper cups was long gone, except for the few that had missed the trashcan nearby. No one said a word to me as I fixated on the forsaken paper cups.

I figured the coach knew the game of basketball better than me, he must have had his reasons. *Could I really be that bad? Or had he forgotten there were two of us again?*

The scoreboard hit the two-minute mark when our coach started subbing out the starters. You know the drill. With every break in play, a benchwarmer took the court so that the star players had a moment of applause from the crowd crammed tight in the bleachers. Coach glanced down the bench. My eyes dropped to the dirty wood planks, then to my orange and white freshly-washed uniform—my lucky number thirteen jersey as clean as when I had pulled it from the dryer that morning. The tears welled, but I kept my gaze down. I'm not sure if someone told him or he finally opened his eyes and saw me.

He did the unthinkable.

With twenty seconds left on the clock, he stood up and called my name, waving me over in a panic. "You haven't been in yet?"

I didn't answer, but my perfectly smooth 90s high ponytail gave it away. I wanted to crawl under the bleachers, anything to not step foot on the court. He sent me to the scorekeeper anyway and the ref waved me on. I didn't touch the ball, there wasn't time. The deafening buzzer blasted as a line of zeros froze in place, the scoreboard boasting our victory.

My coach, bless his oblivious heart, came onto the court laughing out loud. His voice boomed throughout the gymnasium, communicating all the excuses in the book. Embarrassment washed over me. I stood there, straight-faced and unflinching. I must have faded into the background because he walked away still chuckling. No real apology, no good explanation. We had won the game, but I had lost every ounce of dignity in the process.

I left the gym that night with my head down, my chest hot and tight. The reservoir of tears edged closer, about to overflow as I walked to our VW Vanagon. No one congratulated me on a game well played. No one sympathized or apologized for what happened. The silence around me amplified my coach's laughter, a careless voice echoing in my lonely soul. I wanted to scream. *What am I, invisible?*

The side door of the van lurched open with the pull of the handle. Sliding across the back bench seat, I closed my eyes and felt two silent tears run down my shadowed face. I longed for one of my family members to address the oversized elephant riding shotgun on my mother's lap. It's not that I needed a pep-talk or advice. I needed to be seen. I needed a hug and a shoulder to cry on, to not feel so alone.

I crawled into bed as soon as dinner ended. The play-by-play commentary drifted down the hall from the kitchen as my dad and Brenda discussed the game highlights. An overwhelming sense of loneliness came over me, feeling as if my few seconds on the basketball court equaled my net worth. My throat burned as the tears came fast and hard.

My coach had forgotten me.

My family had forgotten me.

Maybe God had forgotten me, too.

My basketball days were over after that season. I never mentioned the game or how I felt. I wanted to forget about it forever. The memory hid itself away for a very long time. I learned that silence is a killer to the soul—more damaging than an awkward conversation any day. Silence doesn't make the memory go away, it just buries the hurt deep into our hearts. So deep it's hard to unearth.

Feeling forgotten stinks.

If I had a more intimate relationship with God during my teen years, it might have been a different story. Maybe I would have known that He saw me no matter how invisible or forgotten I felt. Maybe I would have expressed my disappointment with honesty. Instead, the silence I embraced only made the loneliness grow. The feeling of not good enough became a belief I couldn't shake.

That all changed years later on another tear-filled night. I sat in the bleachers on a college campus waiting for Brenda to play her first collegiate volleyball game. We hadn't seen each other for weeks and the tears flowed freely as she ran out of the locker room wearing my number thirteen on her back. *Why would she change her jersey number?* I wondered.

After the game, Brenda explained. "I'm starting to see the power of humility in your lucky number thirteen. Your spirit is with me every time I put on this jersey." Playing college ball far from home, with extremely talented players, put her in my athletic shoes for the first time ever. She cried her share of tears during tryouts, doubted her abilities at times, and worked hard to earn playing time. In the course of a few months, she understood me better than ever before. She finally grasped how difficult my high school experience had been. Personal experience usually develops into clarity.

We talked about that freshman basketball game, how she wished it could have been different. Breaking years of silence reprogrammed a false belief of mine, God was ever-present even when I felt invisible to the world. *I know the God who sees me.* Back then, I was focused on success and making an impact on the court—being seen by the people around me. But God didn't care about any of that, He wanted to increase my dependency on Him.

Since that day, I've learned an important lesson. If I'm feeling unseen by the people around me—people who love me but just don't know how to show it in the moment, I need to speak up. I need to ask for help or for a hug. Vulnerability with God and others creates community. It's hard to feel alone when people know what's going on inside of you. In intense situations, it can be difficult for me to remember the lessons I've learned in the past. At times, I've reverted back to the fourteen-year-old girl feeling alone and unseen.

There will be circumstances in life much more heartbreaking than a high school basketball game: times when death steals, hearts break, and wrongs are swept under the rug. The people around me may not know how to respond. They won't always know what to do or say when the fires of life are blazing hot. Words fail us at times, and they fail the people who love us. It's not that they don't care, they just don't always recognize what's going on around them. Like the time my husband couldn't see the bird right in front of us, and then it showed off all its red-tailed glory.

Above all else, I've learned there is Someone who will never fail me. He comforts me in my darkest moments and reminds me how loved I am. His love is better than the win, better than the playing time. Better than all the applause of a packed gymnasium. No matter what happens in the game of life, whether I'm in the starting lineup or sitting on the sidelines, God sees me.

The question is this: can I see Him in the midst of pain and suffering? When I feel alone will I choose to look up?

The Long Way Back

Grace carries us through the unknown.

Our stuffed packs were sandwiched in a row on the backseat, like plump sausages ready to grill. I had agreed to tag along with three of my guy friends for a week in the wilderness. Eighteen years old and a bit cocky. We didn't anticipate a three-hour delay on the way to the trailhead, it should have been a sign of things to come. Nevertheless, our inflated confidence—or maybe our ignorance—matched our stuffed packs.

We met at the Ventana Wilderness trailhead, near Big Sur, California. The original idea was to hit the trail by early afternoon and arrive by dinnertime to eat and setup camp. As we pulled into the rocky parking lot, the butterflies in my stomach swarmed. Being the only girl in the group didn't bother me during the planning stages, but now that our adventure was about to start my hesitation grew. The guys joked and laughed in between unloading all the gear and using the last real restroom, a drop-toilet outhouse.

Anxious to get going, Dan barked out orders to our crew. "It's time to move, folks. We're running late as it is."

The postponed start time was threatening our plans for a

celebratory supper. We had set our hearts on a real feast instead of the freeze-dried camping meals for at least that first night. Each of us contributed a special item, a splurge if you will.

Dan, the youngest but most experienced backpacker of the group, tucked a watermelon under his arm, holding it like a football. Bryan, my lanky good friend, packed in four russet potatoes covered with foil for roasting, and his guitar. What's a campfire without some music? Noland supplied the protein: two cans of Dennison's chili. I took charge of making dessert—a boxed no-bake cheesecake. A tin pie plate rested on the very top of my gear.

I hoisted the huge, army green, borrowed backpack onto my shoulders, buckled the waist strap and cinched it tight. I had crammed in all the necessary items to get me through six nights in the wilderness: food, clothing, cooking supplies, a sleeping bag, flashlight, water filter, and a roll of toilet paper. The visions of prancing around my living room the night before instantly fled as the awkward load rested on my twiggy frame. Before even setting foot on the trail, my mind questioned if I could support the heavy pack for the next six miles.

The sun, still high overhead, beat down and pierced our eyes, disguising the time. We set out at a fast pace, adrenaline pumping through our young legs. Navigating the pine-needle-covered trail came easy at first as we climbed over fallen tree trunks and ascended the switchbacks.

At the top of the ridge, the trail opened to a clearing. We stopped to catch our breath and scanned the horizon, a sea of redwoods mixed with pine. Absolutely gorgeous. I leaned against a nearby stump, repositioning the weight of my pack. Thirty pounds felt like eighty digging into my hips. *What have I gotten myself into?* Despite the sweat-soaked shoulder straps digging deep into my sore trapezoids, the vast beautiful forest beckoned us to continue.

We trudged on until our growling stomachs forced us to stop.

Dan, our bossy trail guide, grabbed a granola bar from the side zipper of his pack. He spoke up in a gruff voice and kept moving. "No time to stop. I don't know how much longer, but we have to make it to the stream."

The sun had disappeared and a damp cold fog crept over us. Soon it would be completely dark. We didn't know how far we'd come or how much farther we had to go, but I knew hiking in the dark is never a good idea. I tried not to think of anything scary: wild animals, strange mountain men, or falling from a cliff. The rumblings of my stomach imitated the sounds of a growling bear. Suddenly juicy watermelon and cheesecake didn't seem so important.

Our only concern was making it safely to our destination—a freshwater stream at the end of the trail. My eyes and ears scanned the surrounding darkness, fixed on finding that stream. I pulled out a bag of beef jerky, figuring if I ate the whole thing then my pack would be twelve ounces lighter.

Bryan and I exchanged concerned glances, fearing that our first backpacking experience may very well be the last. Trying to conserve the batteries of our flashlights, we forced our eyes to adjust to the shadows of blackness and even adopted a strange glow-in-the-dark caterpillar as our pet mascot. The fuzzy creature rested in an empty plastic water bottle tied to the front strap of Bryan's pack. In a small way, the faint glow inspired us to keep walking.

Just when it seemed I couldn't take another step, the distant sound of running water trickled past my ears. Relief swept over me. The dark trail didn't seem so scary with the sound of the stream to guide us. The melody of moving water led us along and eventually brought us to our journey's end. The trail stopped at the stream, moonlight dancing on ripples of water. *Hallelujah, we made it!*

Exhausted, we collapsed to the ground. Peeling off our packs, we rolled out our sleeping bags and conked out. No one moved a muscle until the sun peeked from between the trees and woke us with the full force of daybreak.

I opened my eyes and looked around. Three colorful lumps were sprawled out at random, the contents of our packs scattered. I pulled my portable stove from the front zipper of my pack and before long, steam rose from the blue-speckled kettle and the boys started waking up. There wasn't much to say at first. We circled up, each of us clutching our tin cups of cocoa.

Bryan broke the silence. "That was quite a night."

All of our heads nodded in sluggish agreement.

"Dreadful is a better description of what we endured last night. We could have run into all kinds of trouble." I said it without much emotion and then my panicky mind thought about the hike back to our cars. "You guys think the way back will be any easier?"

Dan piped up. "Nope. The first two miles, we climbed up over the ridge, remember all the switchbacks? Then four down to the stream. The way back is gonna be even tougher."

We sat there looking at the fire, letting the hard facts sink like a stone in the river. Then we moved on like eighteen-year-olds do: we set up camp, found a swimming hole, and gathered firewood to prepare our celebratory dinner feast—a day late but still as tasty.

When all the food was gone, I jumped up from my place at the campfire to fetch the cheesecake resting on a rock in the cold stream. The filling set perfectly, with a ring of golden graham cracker crust around the edges. I scooped a fourth of a pie onto each of our plates.

Dan took a bite, then cleared his throat. "What if we didn't go back the way we came?"

The rest of us gave him a confused look and he went on.

"This stream runs through a campground on its way to the ocean. What if we followed the water downstream, let it take us back to the main highway. We can find a way back to our cars."

Not take the trail. Are you kidding me? This is not a good idea.

My thoughts flew through my mind. My throat went dry. I didn't object or even speak, let alone eat my cheesecake. I followed the conversation without contributing my opinion because what could I say without revealing the uneasiness racing through me. It didn't take long for them to make up their minds. All three of them agreed. I was the odd man out in more ways than one.

I gathered the plates and headed down to the stream, my trembling hands and knotted stomach fearing the worst. By the time the rinsed dishes lay on a nearby rock, my spirit had settled. The sound of the flowing water reminded me that God would be with us. The stream would be there to guide us on an unknown adventure towards home.

We played for a few days and made more memories than I could ever share, but every day closer to the long way back made me more jittery. My thoughts couldn't dismiss the anxiety of what laid ahead. The plan was set: we'd give ourselves two full days to reach the campground in case we ran into trouble along the way.

With no clear path to follow, every curve in the stream revealed a new obstacle to navigate. Being on level ground and carrying lighter packs helped. The mental challenge outweighed the physical this time around. We hiked what felt like forever until the wooded trees shied away. The path ended at a small sandy beach. We couldn't go any further. Two walls of granite rose high above our heads. I said what everyone was thinking.

"Now what do we do? We never should have come this way."

Dan set down his pack, unconcerned. "Let's camp here

tonight. We've come too far to go back now, and besides this beachside campsite is more than ideal."

My shoulders slumped and a deep sigh left my mouth. Yielding to uncertainty has never been my strong suit, back then or even now.

The next morning, a pile of logs tied with fishing line was moored on the riverbank. Dan had been up for hours rigging up a raft right out of the classic movie, *Swiss Family Robinson*. After breakfast and breaking camp, we piled our packs at the edge of the pebbled shoreline. The rock walls hovered over us, measuring ten feet high and at least twice that in length. Beyond the calm water, we could see a worn path hidden amongst the trees downstream. If we couldn't go around the water, then we'd have to go straight through it.

Visions of Moses and the Red Sea filled my mind, us swimming through water with walls of granite on either side, while God's people walked on dry ground with walls of water. *Is this how the Israelites felt fleeing Egypt?*

The raft couldn't hold all the weight, so we swam one pack through the deep water at a time. Each of us manned a side and did our best to keep the make-shift barge from sinking. We were soaked, but four mostly dry packs are better than wet packs any day.

We whooped in excitement upon reaching the other side and left our contraption of logs for another weary hiker. The success fueled our energy, and we slung our packs over our dripping bodies, hoping our destination would be near. Before long, the sound of rushing water roared in the distance. We pressed on, unable to decipher what lay ahead besides the thunderous sound of crashing water. The longer we hiked, the louder the thundering became.

Out of nowhere, a bright orange blow-up innertube caught my

attention. A dark-haired barefoot boy weaved through the trees with a giddy grin on his face. The stream turned, revealing a whole crew of children holding colorful floaties. They waited for a turn down a rockslide and into the pool below.

I think we scared the kids, us coming out of nowhere looking like ragged vagabonds. They let us go first down the rock ahead of them, staring with wide eyes as we held our packs on our laps and slipped down the natural water slide. Drenched and relieved to find civilization, we trudged through the campground and hiked two miles up the highway to our parked cars.

Whether it be backpacking through the wilderness or trekking through adversity, I've experienced grace throughout the unknowns of my life. When those granite walls felt impassible, the sandy beach provided us time and rest to move on. The *how* is rarely clear in the moment. That's when listening comes in real handy. I discovered that God's grace can be found in the trickling stream *and* in the thunderous rushing river. It emerges from the most unlikely places, shows up when we are ready to quit or turn back.

Grace is found in the quiet whisper, in the signs painted across the sky, and in the faint sound of water growing with each step we take. Grace walks with us and even carries us if necessary.

I need to remember this especially now, and in the future. The second half of a journey, the second half of life, could be an uphill climb. Grace carries us through the unknown and helps us face the future with courage.

Maggots

Grace values good intentions.

Returning to my dorm room between classes, I unlocked my door, peering hopefully around the corner to our couch.

"Jen, you'll never guess."

Jen looked up as I dropped my backpack to the floor. "What?"

I rolled my eyes, handing over the yellow mailroom notice.

She held the slip of paper up close, trying to decipher it through the smudges and stickiness. "Undeliverable package … from Hawaii? Who sent it?"

I gave her a knowing smirk and pressed my lips together. "Take a guess."

"No way. Why couldn't they deliver it?"

"Apparently, the mailroom staff showed up this morning to a bin of mail covered in maggots. The disgusting little things were eating their way through the plastic padded envelope addressed to me from a Hawaiian FedEx station."

"Maggots? What the heck did he send?"

"Who knows. They didn't dare open it. The whole thing ended up in the trash. If it was any other week I might laugh."

Jen handed the notice back to me, her compassionate smile vanished as she looked down at her palms, disgusted. She disappeared into the bathroom, turned on the water, and lathered up her hands with soap. "You sure know how to pick 'em. You think if he comes back, it'll work out between you two?"

I imagined my boyfriend on a beach in Hawaii trying to come up with a spontaneous souvenir to send. He was sweet but lacked common sense at times. "After this fiasco, what do *you* think?

Later, the phone rang and Jen picked up. I hoped it might be my mom checking in again. After my grandmother's unexpected passing, I'd been emotional all week.

"Hello…. Yeah, she's here. Hold on a sec." Jen stretched the six-foot-long cord across the room to where I sat at my desk. She covered the receiver and whispered, "I think it's him."

My eyes darted back and forth nervously. *Why in the world is he calling? Wasn't the maggot-y package enough?* I took a deep breath, trying to prepare myself for a conversation I'd rather not have.

"Hello." It came out dryer than I intended.

"Hey, you. Did you get my package? Wasn't the fish beautiful?" His voice boomed through the receiver, hurried and excited to hear my response.

"A package? You sent a fish? Well, that explains the maggots then." The line fell silent.

"Maggots? Wait a minute, you didn't get the fish? Oh … shoot." He went into an elaborate story of excuses and explaining. Fishing on a gorgeous beach. Reeling in a tropical beauty. Wishing I could see it. Missing me. "Are you mad?"

This guy was larger than life, spontaneously amusing. I'd never dated anyone who challenged my sense of adventure the way he did. Unpredictably fun. Until it wasn't. His seize-the-day mentality had come back to bite him more times than I could count. He meant well, but disaster seemed to follow him. Everywhere.

"I'm not mad. It's just that your package didn't come at the best time. My grandmother's memorial service is Monday. Car accident."

A hush came over the line. I could tell he didn't know how to respond. "Oh, Wendi... I'm so sorry. About your grandmother. About the fish. I really messed up."

I shook my head in disbelief, a half-smile turned into a chuckle as I tried to put the pieces together. "You sent me a fish? In the mail? From Hawaii? What were you thinking?"

"Apparently, I wasn't. Maybe a painted coconut would have turned out better...and less maggot-y."

"Yeah, next time send me a painted coconut."

<hr>

After five short months of dating this guy, I'd come to realize first-hand that meaning well and turning out well are not one and the same. His good intentions didn't always work out. I didn't hold it against him when he took me surfing on a longboard nicknamed "The Bruised Banana." It wasn't pretty: the board, my novice surfing skills, or my bloody shins walking back to the car. I never blamed him for the rollerblading incident either, even though he knew I had endured a neck injury as a kid. The smooth halls of the elementary school served as the ultimate backdrop for our game of tag in the dark. After skating full speed into a chain, I became one with the cement. Then he up and moved to Hawaii and thought sending dead animals in the mail was a good idea.

The fish was just another well-meaning display of his audacious spirit. An opportunity for me to focus on his good intentions, not the outcome, and definitely not the maggots. We didn't stay together much longer, but it wasn't because of the well-meaning-gift-gone-bad. The fishy package will always be a story to remember. A story of the time when I valued someone's good intentions more than the outcome.

Sometimes grace is the only appropriate response. I know I need it, so then how can I possibly refuse to extend it to others? Blunder after blunder, more grace. Every mistake and misjudgment—grace. Grace for me and grace for others. Grace for the failures and bad decisions. Grace for the maggots of life that spring out of nowhere. When our best laid plans fail miserably, grace sweeps up the pieces. God has swept up the pieces in my life. Every time.

We all need more generous grace than what we expect to receive. Especially college guys who think sending a fish in the mail is a good idea. Grace is willing to see past the maggots of life. To see the good in every person and situation as often as possible.

Seven Dollars Cash

Grace in any denomination
makes a huge impact.

I slid my debit card through the terminal as the checker in a red polo loaded up a plastic bag with toothpaste, laundry detergent, and a pack of colored notecards. I'm convinced colored notecards got me through college. They were worth every penny, even when I didn't have a penny to spare.

The register groaned a low note and the checker responded in a monotone voice. "Denied. Do you want to try it again?"

I gulped in dismay. It had never happened before, and I didn't know what to do. I bit my lip and mentally scanned the bank of my memory. *This seriously can't be happening. I never should have bought those cute shoes.* I swiped the card again, hoping for the best but the lady in red raised her eyebrows and gave me a disappointed look. She waited as I reached into my wallet and handed over my last twenty-dollar bill. I retrieved the change and walked out deflated and feeling overwhelmed by responsibility.

Living on my own for eight months out of the year had its advantages. I loved everything about college life: the independence, the friendships, the psychology courses. My part-time job on campus kept me afloat between volleyball season and the end of spring semester. Then I worked my butt off all summer to save every penny so that this very thing wouldn't happen. Two years of college under my belt, two to go. Maybe my approach needed to change.

Driving back to my dorm room, I cleared my mind of every negative thought. No amount of scolding would fix my problem. I needed a game plan, a way to stretch my last few dollars to my next paycheck. A strategy slowly formed in my mind. *If I don't drive anywhere, I'll be good on gas. Thank goodness I can eat all my meals in the cafeteria. And no shopping, whatsoever!* Adulting in college taught me some serious life skills. I'm still as thrifty as a church mouse on a budget.

The next morning after class, I moseyed into the mail room. I had tried to be my perky self since the scenario in Target, but the recession of my bank account had me a bit frazzled. *I've got to start balancing my checkbook every week.* I fumbled with my key ring and crouched down to reach box number 326. Surprised, I pulled out an envelope addressed to me with my mom's familiar handwriting. I fist pumped the air as the key turned to lock the square metal door. Getting mail in college was as exciting as Christmas.

The paper shell flew off before I even left the mailroom. Inside, I found a cute note from Mom and seven dollars cash. So unexpected. *She's never sent money to me before. I wonder how she knew?* I nearly cried as I walked to my dorm room, an ear-to-ear smile on my now hope-filled face.

My parents would have loved to support me financially, but they couldn't swing it. Four daughters, three of them in college, on a mailman's salary. I'm not sure how my mother knew I was running on empty, her small but generous gift infused hope into my seemingly desperate situation. It wasn't much, but it helped me put a few gallons of gas in my tank and a couple bucks in my pocket.

At the time, my limited perspective blocked the ability to have

God-centered vision. I attributed the seven dollars to mere happenstance. A sweet motherly gesture. But now I see it. I see grace written across George Washington's wide forehead. I see God's kindness stamped in green just below IN GOD WE TRUST.

God strengthens my faith every time He acts on my behalf. Every time He blesses me with gifts and even when the blessing comes in the form of a hard lesson learned, it's for my ultimate good.

After twenty-plus years, I know now that grace doesn't have to come in big proportions to make a huge impact. Even seven measly dollars turns up as God's provision. Like how a bird landing on my car at the perfect moment changed me forever. How could something so seemingly insignificant make all the difference? I want to remember this and see it more often, without having to adjust my perspective. What if I lived every day expecting to see the smallest bits of grace all around me?

In God's economy, He takes the small stuff and multiplies it like no one else. He provided help when I least expected it and cemented a sense of dependency in me that has lasted a lifetime. Supplying hope to the hopeless is always a big deal, no matter what denomination it comes in.

Like succulents in my garden, God propagates blessing in a variety of ways. Jesus turned water to wine, he miraculously filled a boat with fish, and He multiplied seven loaves of bread to feed a crowd of thousands. In the case of my seven dollars, it wasn't a multiplication of funds but of faith. After far too long, my eyes have been opened.

My mom's small offering ignited hope in me. Her gift increased my faith. The size of the gift was irrelevant. The impact, incomprehensible. Training my eyes to see His grace has taken a lifetime of studying and reflecting on the goodness of God. I'm collecting each moment and storing them in my heart.

Notecards optional.

The Ring

Grace exceeds our wildest dreams.

I gasped as Josh got down on one knee—we had started dating six months after the episode with the maggots and been together for two years. There'd been not a hint of spontaneity with this fellow, until that very moment. He pulled out a tiny drawstring bag, a quiver in his voice.

"Wendi, will you marry me?"

He slid the ring onto my finger. Speechless, I looked down at my hand. *Goodness gracious, it's beautiful.* Like no ring I had ever seen or imagined. The thick band of white gold anchored the two oblong rectangles of yellow that framed a recessed square diamond. Subtle and alluring. Looking closer, I noticed a design etched in the rectangles of yellow gold, like a fan of three curved leaves. This was no ordinary ring, it had history written all over it.

"I love it…. Where did you find this?" My eyes finally left the newly occupied finger and searched Josh's giddy eyes filled with tears of joy.

"It's a long story. I wish my 'Greempa' could see your face right now—my dad's dad. The ring belonged to him, and now it's yours."

"It's perfect. I love everything about it, especially that it was your grandfather's. I couldn't have chosen a more beautiful ring." The words came out slow and contemplative as my gaze returned to the circle of gold, shaking my head in wonder.

"If you'd rather put the diamond in a new setting we can."

"Not in a million years, you silly man. It's beyond my wildest dreams." I kissed his right check, then his left. "Yes."

A few months earlier, Josh was home for Thanksgiving break. The topic of marriage had come up more than a few times between the two of us, and even with his parents. Josh isn't one to divulge many details, but my mother in-law had no problem filling me in. As he sat with his parents at the kitchen table after dinner one night, the conversation began.

"We know you love her. So, what's holding you back, Son?" Josh's mom, Joette, asked the open-ended question and then paused, waiting for him to articulate his response.

"No ring.... No money for a ring. How can I propose without one?" I imagine the disappointment in his voice tinged with defeat.

Joette looked at her son, now a grown man, with a knowing smile. She realized the issue didn't matter in the long run, but to him it was a deal-breaker. Just then a solution formed in her mind. "What if I had a ring?" The words stumbled out of her mouth in excitement.

Josh's eyes lit up as Joette hurried upstairs to her bedroom. She returned holding a small silk bag with a drawstring. I envision the verse from the book of Ephesians coming to life as he slowly opened the elegant pouch and the ring dropped into his hands: sometimes God gives us more than all we ask or imagine. Sometimes His grace exceeds our wildest dreams. Josh stared in disbelief at the ring, then gently set it down and looked at his mother in shock.

"It was Greempa's—his pinky ring. You're more than welcome to it, like it is or use the diamond in a new setting."

I see him looking down at the ring now resting on the antique cherry-wood table, a spark of hope filling the room. "Are you sure? How can I accept such a gift? Really, Mom, it's too much."

Joette beamed with delight. "Of course, I'm sure. You need a ring and we have one. Someone should be wearing it. Who better than Wendi? We're just as crazy about her as you are."

A soft determined smile settled over Josh's face, his mind picturing a perfect moment not far into the future. He was ready.

God regularly gives us more than we ask or even imagine. I've seen it again and again. I've heard thousands of stories about His unending love, His generous grace. There have been countless beautiful moments leading to new adventures in my life. Even my hardest stories have revealed a sliver of grace hidden inside. The opportunities that have come my way after heartache are evidence of His kindness. When I consider the goodness of God, that circle of gold placed on my finger is another example of grace. Grace given to Josh, and then given to me, too.

Jesus shows up and goes beyond what I would ever think to ask for. He did it in the pages of Scripture and He's done it in my life, too. If we dare to discover the beauty of grace, He exceeds our wildest dreams.

Over twenty-five years later, I still catch myself gazing at my beautiful ring. A ring that pays tribute to Josh's Greempa—his Chinese heritage on my finger. A ring that reminds me of his selfless parents, willing to help in any way they could.

My gorgeous ring is a symbol of our simple beginnings as a

couple. Of our blossoming love at the start of our journey together. The ring has led to so much more: a loving extended family, children of our own, and a partner who has stuck by me even when the road has been harder than I ever imagined.

Now, even more than back then, what it represents is beyond my wildest dreams.

Wedding Shoes

Grace challenges man-made traditions.

S omething old, something new. Something borrowed, something blue.

Old, new, and borrowed. I had those three elements figured
out in the early months of 1999, six months before my Big
Day. But the *something blue* really had me stumped. I didn't
want a blue-ribboned garter or a sapphire-hued hair accessory.
Handkerchiefs didn't speak to me, and blue nail polish seemed
overly gaudy.

Some wedding details require more time to take shape, I'd
been told. My *something blue* would hopefully be revealed before I walked down the aisle. At the time, I didn't have a clue in
the world.

The other mystery revolved around my shoes. Every mall in
Southern California had its share of bridal stores, and we had
visited them all without much luck. Each shop boasted an entire
wall of white wedding shoes embellished in all sorts of ways: lacy
trim, satin bows, glitzy rhinestones.

My face cringed with every pair I tried on. None of them felt
right. The heels made me look too tall, the flats too boring, and
the sandals were too strappy and sparkly. None of them made

my eyes light up. Trying to squeeze into someone else's shoes is never a good move, especially when those shoes are walking down the aisle. I didn't want anything askew on my wedding day, but my options were running out.

After yet another failed shoe excursion in the mall, Josh and I made our way to the parking garage. We passed the final lineup of shops: clothes, leather goods, and jewelry under clear glass. We rounded the corner and he stopped.

"Do you mind if we run over to Champs before we go? I want to pick up some tennis shoes."

"Of course. One of us might as well go home with some new kicks."

We spun around, hand in hand, and made our way to the athletic store. All the sporting goods lined the right side: a ball for every recreational activity, skateboards, and tennis racquets. The left wall displayed baseball hats of every college and pro team in existence.

The cashier asked if we needed any help. We smiled politely and trudged through racks of professional jerseys and workout clothes and sweatpants until we hit the shoe section in the very back. Rows and rows of footwear lined the wall. Walking and running shoes, hiking boots, basketball high-tops, and casual leather sneakers.

Josh headed for the Adidas section. He had his eyes on a new pair of Rod Laver's—white mesh and a suede upper, with a shamrock green accent on the heel. He pulled out the box, tried them on, and walked over to the full-length mirror. I kept myself busy looking at a display of trail shoes when he called my name.

"Hey Wen, what do you think about wearing these to the wedding?"

I turned my head ready to laugh, and instead raised my eyebrows. In his hands he held an Adidas white all-leather shoe, set off just perfectly with a cornflower blue heel highlight—the Stan Smith. Unlike other Adidas shoes, the Stan Smith does not feature the customary three bold stripes. It walks to a different beat—kind of like me.

Apparently, Stan Smith was a legendary tennis player from the 1970's. The iconic, elegantly simple shoe had survived the test of time and decked out millions of feet over the years. But had it ever adorned a bride walking down the aisle? My heart skipped a beat, and I bit my lip in contemplation. *Could I really wear sneakers to my wedding? What would my grandmother say?*

Josh's eyes lit up as I cocked my head and paused, relieved to think that the end of the search could soon be over. He scanned the pile from the ground up, his pointer finger running along the sizes on the tall tower of shoe boxes. It stopped on the last one. He picked it up and peeked inside before holding it out towards me.

My perfect size sat right on top, could it be a sign? I never imagined finding my *something blue* in a pair of leather athletic shoes or having the boldness to wear the unexpected. Back then, sneakers were a far cry from conventional wedding attire. *What the heck?*

We left the mall smiling, both of us, the bright blue box tucked under my arm. My Stan Smith's stole the conversation on the ride home—the last piece of the wedding puzzle solved. Josh reveled that I would go against the grain of tradition and not let it define me. He said the bride could wear whatever shoes suited her fancy.

Weddings naturally allow for this uniqueness. The dress, the flowers, the venue—solely chosen by the bride, and in my case, the groom, too. Other aspects of my life don't embrace this liberty so easily. I tend to listen to people and culture more than I should, dictating what I wear and watch and value. I have to constantly remind myself that I look to God for acceptance, not the people around me. It takes fortitude to shine in a dark place and courage to walk with confidence when the world begs us to blend in.

Even spiritual traditions can overlook the heart of God. Throughout the Scriptures, the religious leaders missed it big-time—the ones who walked alongside the promised Messiah. Our churches are no different. We often hold onto our preconceived ideas and disregard how Jesus loved imperfect people. I've seen how grace challenges man-made traditions—how it seeks to discover God's flawless perspective of humanity.

I've seen how grace lets people embody their quirky awesome selves. Wedding day or not, I can dazzle the people around me when I'm reflecting God's goodness. When I'm living out who I was made me to be I can't help but shine. When I slip on kindness and gentleness and self-control, going against the grain of culture, His light shines through me. Without grace to be myself, I'm just a girl following the crowd. A girl walking around in someone else's shoes.

Like my Stan Smith's, the age-old wedding rhyme has stood the test of time. Even after 150 years, the four good luck objects remain a recipe of tradition for brides everywhere. But that doesn't mean being stuffed into a square box like every other head-over-heels-in-love girl. I had the freedom to decide what to wear and how to shine my brightest self.

The shoes glowed just as intensely on our wedding day, and yet, there's always some who challenge our decisions, who can't imagine a way other than what is expected. Even at the wedding, when I was the star of the day, disapproval threatened my brightness.

After being announced man and wife, Josh and I wandered around the crowd of friends and family. Everyone wanted to steal a moment with us before the reception began. Out of the corner of my eye I saw my grandmother. I felt a confident urge well up within me to show her my shoes. *Oh boy, here goes nothing. I wonder what she'll say.*

"You look so beautiful, Winnie." My grandmother gave me a kiss' on the cheek and stood back to admire my head-to-toe profile.

Like a little girl, I spun around in my dress. Animated and giddy. "Did you see my shoes Grandma?" I was playing with fire, but a growing confidence soared within me.

I raised my knee, revealing the white leather sneakers. Her hand gripped my forearm firmly as I balanced on my teetering straight leg. The adorable fold-over cotton socks with dangling buttons from my childhood couldn't be ignored. But all she could do was gasp.

"Where are your pantyhose and heels? Criminy, no hose under a wedding dress, that's unbelievable." She shook her head and murmured under her breath, "What's this world coming to?"

I giggled and wrapped her in a big hug, whispering into her wrinkly ear, "I love you too, Grandma."

I loved those Stan Smith's with all my heart. That love dictated my decision, not a set of rules or expectations. When Love—the person, not the idea—dictates our decisions, we can champion the unexpected. Living under the umbrella of grace empowers us to love the people around us so they can be the unique individuals God created them to be.

Established traditions are hard to break. People don't always know how to distinguish between what's always been done and what's up for grabs. Grace allows us to be brave mavericks who aren't afraid to go against the tide of tradition, even when the opposition is a sweet but opinionated grandmother.

Embracing our own gutsy ways of living takes courage and it

won't always be acceptable to some. Thankfully, we don't have to live by the standards of tradition. Our hearts thrive when He gets the glory. One *something blue* decision at a time.

Silly Girls

Grace allows laughter to ease heartache.

There we were. The three of us, in the sunny corner of Grandma's living room, sitting on the edge of her hospital bed.

Despite the name I'd given her, Camilla wasn't my grandmother. The eighteen months of caring for her during late-stage Alzheimer's disease changed that in a snap. Robbed of her memories, or quite possibly the ability to frame them, Camilla's daily needs proved to be a challenge for her loving family. Brenda and I stepped in to help, providing around-the-clock care. We were both married, in our early twenties before children entered the scene, and Grandma was nearing eighty-seven years young at the time.

Grandma sat in the middle, Brenda on one side of her and me on the other. We're counting. "One … two … three."

Her wheelchair, angled and braked, stood ready for the coordinated move, but uncontrollable laughter stopped us before we could stand up. We couldn't keep it together for more than two minutes before another round swept in. The laughter gave way to real-life tears rolling down our cheeks. An ordinary sheet-change couldn't be that funny, but our giggles wouldn't let up.

It didn't faze Grandma, though. She waited patiently with a far-off gaze, patting her lap and nervously adjusting the elastic band around her waist, busy as a toddler, her mind trapped in an ailing body. Content to sit there all day, she wasn't in a hurry. Neither were we.

I'd done it a hundred times before, transporting her to the chair on wheels, usually alone. But that afternoon, Brenda and I were having a marvelous time together.

With Grandma sandwiched between us, we tried again. Each of us gently gripped one delicate forearm. Brenda swept her smile away and changed her tone, determined to reset our focus. "Okay, let's try it again. On three."

The laughter erupted just as we leaned forward in one fluid motion, only to sink back onto the white sheets. Giggling like schoolgirls. *How is it that tears fall more easily while laughing than crying?*

Grandma sighed and rubbed her eyebrow. "You silly girls." She said it with such candor, as confident as a doctor giving a diagnosis. Mindful of the details and accepting our senseless chitchat with poise, Grandma waited for us to compose ourselves. Our snickering stopped dead in its tracks. My wide eyes met Brenda's in shock, then shifted to the weathered face busy inspecting the loose seam on the cuff of her turtleneck.

"Grandma, I think you've been holding out on us. You know exactly what's going on." I told her pointedly. Her gaze remained unchanged, staring off into the distance.

I've heard it said there's no greater loss than a loved one who doesn't know you. To witness the mental decline of someone you love is more than most families can bear.

For us, we never knew Camilla in her prime. We embraced her just as she was. Gentle and kind, as she talked in endless circles. Feisty when she refused to eat my cooking and forever grateful when I caved to a bowl of strawberry ice cream instead. Sophisticated, the way she fiddled with her hair as if looking in a mirror. Confused, sometimes to the point of tears.

Grandma taught me how to live well. How to be a more engaged observer and to accept how life unfolds in all the various stages. She modeled how to stay joyful even in the hard seasons, and to realize that in every life well-lived there's laughter mixed with tears. Sometimes we laugh so hard we cry, and even tears can turn to laughter as we reminisce about the special moments with those we love.

I loved Camilla with all my heart. The heaviness of her death, but also learning to embrace a soft acceptance, changed me forever. The book of Proverbs speaks of laughter having the ability to camouflage a heavy heart. I always think of Grandma when I read that verse. When laughter ceases … yes, grief remains, but isn't it a little more beautiful to behold? Doesn't laughter ease the heartache that can wear us down?

Now that I think of it, I believe Grandma taught me how to die, too. Gracefully and slowly. There's no rushing the effects of a disease. No sense in trying to predict how long we have left. Only God knows when it's time to meet our Maker.

After finding her, cold and rigid, one December morning, the hospice nurse encouraged Brenda and me to savor our last few hours with Camilla. "You'll never get these moments back. Don't be scared and don't rush it."

Nervous at first, we held Grandma's hands and told stories while changing her into a fresh nightgown. Then we washed her face for the last time. The memories kept spilling out, a mess of tears as we stood over her. Tears gave way to soft smiles, a quiet internal happiness at the beauty of it all. She had finished well, and we had the amazing privilege to be there at the end. Unthinkable grace.

We spent the rest of the day together, grieving and working. We gathered Grandma's clothes, packed up the kitchen, and a few knick-knacks. Donated it all to hospice. A clean sweep can be invigorating to an emotionally exhausted spirit. The closure felt good, like the feeling after a good hard laugh. I went home, hugged my husband, and pondered what I would do next. *What could possibly fill Grandma's place in my grieving heart?*

A few days later, the funeral home called. "We need a set of clothes for Camilla to be buried in. Since there isn't going to be a viewing, anything will do. But maybe not her nightgown."

Brenda and I burst into laughter, kicking ourselves for giving away every article of clothing in Camilla's closet. "Guess it's time to go shopping for Grandma," I concluded.

Too quick to the punch, I guess we got ahead of the process. So out to the mall, we went. It turned out to be an amusing shopping excursion trying to find a suitable outfit for our dear Camilla. We laughed, explaining the whole scenario to the friendly sales associate helping us pick out a flowered blouse and coordinating pants. The laughter filled a bit of the emptiness in my heart, eased the grief a little.

Now, years later, I see the tenderness of what happened. The mishap gave us one last outing together to serve Grandma. I like to think she was watching from heaven, laughing too. It makes me want to laugh louder and longer. To giggle when grace shows up in surprising ways. To stand in awe of the beauty of grace.

Flip The Cards

Grace knows when it's okay to say no.

I come from a game-playing family. Uno, charades, Rummikub—you name it, we've played it. Of all the games in our game closet, I've never been a fan of *Monopoly*. Even as a child, I'd choose cards or checkers, anything but the vicious strategy of forcing opponents into bankruptcy. *Monopoly* has the strange ability to get personal from the get-go. It always seems to end with too many hotels, not enough money, and hurt feelings. Nevertheless, one evening during Family Game Night at my parents' house, my two brothers-in-law coaxed me into playing. I tried every excuse to resist, but somehow, they talked me into it.

"Come on, Wendi, you know you want to." Adam joked.

I raised my eyebrows in protest.

Before I could comment, Lee chimed in. "It'll be fun, and we promise not to get too competitive, right, Adam?"

I was fresh out of excuses, and before I could think up a suitable reason why I couldn't play, the board game appeared. Banker Adam started stacking our lump sums in neat little piles according to denomination on each end of the board. I smiled on the outside, but inside I anticipated trouble ahead.

As we picked out our pieces, I took a deep breath and told myself that it didn't matter where I landed or how much moolah I had to hand over. I reminded myself that play money isn't real. *Wendi, chill out and have fun. It's just a game.*

Once every property had been snatched up, the negotiations began. Trading cards to form monopolies and granting immunities is where it gets ugly. Alliances are forged and the game takes on a whole new tone. My accumulation of weak properties didn't help in the bargaining department. With zero allies, my one purple trio, and two random railroad properties, I didn't stand a chance. As the red hotels slowly started filling the cardboard landscape, I tried to stay calm.

One green property with a hefty rent, "Pacific Avenue", pulled my thimble piece in every single time. I couldn't get around the board without landing on it or one of the other green money makers. Greedy bunch of squares, that's what they were! Even the Community Chest cards rallied against me.

I wanted nothing more than to stand up in protest and dump the board, sending all the pieces flying. But I kept playing. Like being stuck in an elementary school band performance with the only open door on the other side of the auditorium, leaving meant making a scene. I didn't want to let anyone down. Not on Family Game Night.

My husband, Josh, wasn't playing *Monopoly*. He shares my hostility for global property takeover. Instead, he settled on a quiet game of chess. Jealousy burned within me. I would have done anything to be in his shoes. Too bad I never learned about rooks and pawns. *If only I had volunteered to dry the dishes instead of wash them ... then maybe I could have avoided this whole thing!*

Between chess games, Josh walked by the dining room table just as my eyes began to bulge after dishing out another $75 to the Free Parking space. My face must have told the whole story because his dark eyes and gentle smile grabbed my attention. He mouthed the words, "You don't have to play."

At the time, I didn't feel like I had a choice. It was *Monopoly* or nothing, even though the game closet held other options. I could have said no or chosen differently. I could have joined the Yahtzee dice rolling frenzy in the family room. Heck, I could have scooped ice cream and dished out the pie. Why didn't I say, "No, thank you"?

With Josh's words, a realization and relief swept over me. *You're right. I don't have to play. Why do I feel like I do?*

Truth spoken out loud is powerful, even if no one else can hear. It grounded my soul and gave me the determination to stand up for myself. My family wanted to play *Monopoly*, but just because they wanted to play didn't mean it was the best decision for me.

I waited patiently for my turn, playing the scene over in my head more than a few times, trying to bolster my courage to quit. More money landed in the center of the board and a hotel replaced two green plastic houses on Park Place. The perfect time to exit.

I reached out and held the dice in my hand, shaking them as if I was going to roll them onto the square of cardboard. I didn't let them fly though. Instead, I flipped my property cards upside down in one fluid motion. I mortgaged them. Surrendering my measly purple real estate to the highest bidder felt better than winning. Walking away from the *Monopoly* board during Family Game Night was a lesson I desperately needed to learn: Grace knows when it's okay to say no.

People-pleasing has never been a good guide to decision-making. It doesn't work out for me because people-pleasing usually leads to a not-so-great attitude on my part. I get all huffy when all I need to do is say no. Learning to advocate for myself in the small insignificant moments like playing a board game has fueled my confidence to be bold when weightier decisions need to be made. I've seen firsthand that relational decisions have a lot more riding on them than a pile of fake money.

Life isn't a game of *Monopoly.* The stakes are higher, and the consequences can reverberate for months or even years into the future. There have been plenty of times when I put myself in an undesirable situation by voluntarily complying with a reluctant "yes." It could have been avoided if I had the courage to speak up and make the disciplined decision to decline.

Letting go of external expectations has been a gift to my internal being. For me, it's best to steer clear when competition and conflict collide. Oftentimes, declining gracefully is a bold, and necessary, move. And you know what? Everyone survived. My brothers laughed it off and went right back to their schemes of domination. I smiled and took a long deep breath of freedom.

Disappointing my brothers proved to be well worth it.

The fear of letting others down has been a serious issue for me. Becoming a slave to the expectations of people around me is not a smart move, especially when there's more at stake, like my physical and emotional well-being. I'm learning to save my yes responses for the true passions and convictions on my plate, and for the times when God's call is clear and strong. Otherwise, I'm letting grace for myself guide the decision to say no.

Choosing to make decisions out of love not obligation is fundamental in creating time and energy for more of what God has called us to. That still small voice of wisdom is worth listening to.

Big as an Elephant

Grace brings people back together again.

We pulled into the Hollywood Racetrack parking lot—
my mom, Brenda, and me. It was a warm summer day,
the kind of day when your legs stick to the vinyl car seats even
though the AC is on full blast. We had trekked through unexpected traffic on the freeways of Los Angeles resulting in a late
arrival. The engine stopped. I took a deep nervous breath.

"You two ready for this?" The excitement in my mother's
voice couldn't be tamed. After all, she knew these people more
than we did.

With an uncertain smile, I struggled to get out of the backseat,
my pregnant belly protruding farther than what felt appropriate.
I smoothed the wrinkled fabric of my floral maternity skirt and
pulled my tank top a little lower over my middle. There was no
use trying to hide the small bulge of my naval popping out like a
rounded button. *Well, this is as good as it gets.*

We made our way to the counter to check in—a snake of metal
chains like a ride at an amusement park, but completely desert-
ed. We could hear the distant sound of hooves pounding the
track and muffled cheering. I'd never been to a horse race before.
Is this what celebrities do on a Thursday afternoon?

My mom cleared her throat and the attendant whirled around surprised to see us standing there. "We're here for the *Little House on the Prairie* reunion lunch. Is this the correct gate?"

The older woman smiled and looked down at a clipboard. "Well, yes, it is. And who do we have here? Let me guess … you must be Jackie."

My mom grinned with a puzzled expression on her face.

In a half whisper, the attendant leaned towards us. "*Little House* fan, all my life. You two are the last of the cast members to check in. What a thrill to meet Baby Grace." She slid three tiny yellow ribbons across the counter, a straight pin attached to each one. "The horses cross the starting gate in about twenty minutes, that gives you just enough time to get settled for the main event. Your luncheon is located on the Ascot Terrace, overlooking the Winner's Circle. You'll have great seats from there."

My mom smiled and handed each of us a yellow ribbon. We had no idea what to do with it, neither did she. The sidewalk led us to a door and up a flight of metal stairs. Bleachers spanned one side of the track, jam-packed with expectant faces watching as the horses whizzed by. It was loud and rowdy. I felt overdressed and a bit out of place.

We continued through the cheering crowd until we came to a roped off section. A man dressed in a full suit stood guard at the entrance, he wore a top hat.

"Can I help you find what you're looking for? I'm afraid only a yellow ribbon gets you into this area today. Celebrity luncheon."

He touched his lapel, pointing at his own yellow ribbon secured in place. We smiled and held up our ribbons. He nodded and stepped aside, allowing us to enter the landing. We fastened our pins while descending the six steps leading to a platform bustling with servers. A flurry of wild conversation erupted from six round tables filled with unfamiliar faces.

I swallowed hard and did my best to suck in my enormous tummy, I felt as big as an elephant. *Will any of these people remember us? Maybe this wasn't such a good idea.*

A blonde girl with loose ringlets stood up and pointed at us. "Goodness gracious! Baby Grace is having a baby."

I'd heard that voice before … on television. It was none other than the voice of nasty Nellie Oleson. The meanest girl on *Little House* who's actually a sweetheart in real life—Alison Arngrim. She wore a tie-dyed tank top, blue jeans, and a canvas hat. The whole place went quiet.

Karen Grassle (Caroline Ingalls) got out of her seat and hugged my mom. Her eyes filled with tears as she embraced us and put a gentle hand on my swollen belly. Even though Ma's pixie cut seemed foreign to me, her voice sounded the same. "You two are so grown up. How long has it been?"

We looked at my mom, shrugging our shoulders.

"Over twenty-three years since the NBC Goodbye Party. The girls would have been five then."

"And look at you now … having a baby." She turned to Brenda. "What about you?"

"I have two little ones at home. Four and three."

Karen's eyes softened and lit up. "Two busy moms. You both are doing important work, remember that." She looked to her right. "I think there are quite a few people wanting to meet you. Your big sisters are waiting for a hug."

We turned and saw Lindsay and Sydney Greenbush (Carrie Ingalls) grinning from ear to ear. They rushed toward us, laughing, and asking more questions than I would have expected. Like they knew us. They told us how we used to follow them around on location and that our twin photo shoots were some of their favorite memories.

Lindsay's eyes flashed with excitement. "Everyone has been

anticipating your arrival. You could say Baby Grace has been the talk of the town today. Who do you want to see next? Melissa?"

We nodded in agreement as Lindsay led us straight to the star of *Little House on the Prairie*—Melissa Gilbert (Laura Ingalls Wilder).

Melissa gasped and covered her open mouth. "No way my baby sisters could be grown women. Has it been that long?" She told us about sneaking into our dressing room one day and how she taught us our first word while stringing wooden beads on a shoelace.

It felt like a family reunion, sitting around telling stories from the good ol' days. Seeing people from a time you don't remember but they sure do. Everyone was so down to earth and normal. Their warm welcome eased the tension building in my queasy stomach. *How could this be real? I thought celebrities were snooty.... Boy, was I wrong!*

Several cast members never shared the screen with us, but they received Brenda and me just as tenderly as our television family members. The afternoon flew by faster than the horses racing down the track. I was so caught up in conversation I didn't even notice the roar of the crowd as the winning jockey crossed the finish line. He received a gorgeous flower blanket and we all filed down to the track for a photo.

As we were walking back to the terrace, Alison, and her husband Bob, caught up with us. "Looks like you'll be busy for a bit, but maybe you both could break away for a public appearance sometime? Sign some autographs? The fans would love to meet Baby Grace."

I gulped. "You really think so? How fun would that be?"

We said our goodbyes and promised to stay in touch. A warm sensation fell over me—a showering of kindness I didn't expect to receive. My cheeks hurt from smiling and my big belly didn't seem so gargantuan anymore. As we approached the parking lot, I tried to take it all in. Such acceptance, such grace from people we hadn't seen for twenty-three years.

Once again, maybe taking my mind off myself and my insecurities is just what I needed. The graciousness of our TV family helped me see how welcomed we were, regardless of my elephant-sized stomach.

Ending the Blame Game

Grace surrenders the burden of guilt.

On May 8, 2006 I pulled into the driveway at my parents' house. A FOR SALE sign stood in the yard, the word SOLD dancing the mamba in red. The time had come for them to retire, and they chose to trade the California beaches for the hospitality of the South and a lower cost of living.

My mom wasn't home that week. She had traveled to visit her brother across the country, leaving my stepdad alone with more than enough to do. Every room needed to be packed up before escrow closed, so I volunteered to help any chance I got.

After a quick knock, I walked through the front door. My hearty hello found my stepdad in the back bedroom perched on a ladder, his top-half towering into the crawlspace hatch door above the eight-foot ceiling.

Twenty years of odds-and-ends filled a small alcove in the rafters above the guest bedroom. None of the boxes would be going with them, and he wanted to leave every square inch clean for the new owners, so down the boxes came.

"Hey, Wen! You'll never believe what I found up here. Have you been missing any long-lost friends?" He handed down a dusty box for me to open, his dimpled chin exposed a crooked smile.

I saw a porcelain face peering through the worn cardboard, not taped but folded shut. The doll belonged to my older sister, Michelle—one of her prized possessions. She used to prop it up in a sitting position against her pillow, all fancy and beautiful. If the doll slipped down to a horizontal level, her eyelids with those perfectly curled lashes closed until you sat her up again. I pulled the doll out of the box and laid it against my arm. Her blue eyes still opened and closed on their own, but the matted blonde hair and wrinkled velvet dress had long been forgotten.

I set the box down in the corner of the empty room and returned to the bottom of the ladder to grab another, this one filled with dusty picture frames.

"I can email pictures to Michelle, if that would help. She might want to keep the dolls."

Daddy shrugged his shoulders and stopped in midthought. "Maybe she forgot about them. It's a good thing your mother isn't here. She'd say it's all going to the trash."

I gave him a sideways glance and snickered. "How much more is up there? You want help or should I get going on the boat seats from yesterday?"

"I can handle the rest. You've got enough to do."

I headed to the backyard and out to the shop where my project awaited me: a pile of boat seats to clean and reinstall. The heat of the day made the job harder than it needed to be. The sun burned through my tank top. Beads of sweat dripped down to the tips of my elbows. My forehead grew slick with perspiration as I scrubbed the grime from the crevices of the seat.

My dad had been in work clothes earlier, but suddenly he appeared on the deck wearing his swim trunks, bare-chested. He was out of breath. A look of panic gripped his face.

I stopped immediately and led him to the kitchen.

The words fumbled out of his mouth. "Heat stroke … maybe it's heat stroke?"

He sat on a barstool, breathing heavily, while I poured a big glass of ice water and made him a snack. Maybe his blood sugar had tanked. The huffing and puffing continued as I called 911 for advice. The dispatcher offered to send an ambulance, but my dad waved his hand in protest.

"No, I'll be alright. Just need to rest for a bit."

My heart thumped as he laid down on the guest bed, drained of his usual spark. A flurry of questions came out of my mouth. "What have you eaten today? Have you been getting enough sleep with Mom gone? Has this ever happened before?"

He did his best to answer until the snoring started. The loud nasally snarls brought a half-chuckle to my throat. His mouth fell open, his breathing heavy as the fan overhead raced.

My heart rate slowed back to normal. I tiptoed from the room and out to the backyard where I continued with my work. Twice, I peeked my head around the cracked-open door to check on him, but Daddy slept harder than a toddler after a day at the beach.

An hour later, finding another opportunity to pause my work, I again tiptoed toward the room. I leaned my face around the open door and peered inside. Just as before, his mouth was open but this time a deadly silence filled the room. I flew through the door and shook his heavy shoulders trying to revive him, but no breath moved through his nostrils—as still as the dusty porcelain doll. Tears streamed down my face at every failed CPR attempt until the sirens blared up the street and a paramedic stopped me to take over. My dad was gone, and I couldn't do anything to reverse it.

The Blame Game started that day, and it knocks on my door whenever it wants to pester me. It's as though a darkness drags me back to the terrifying moment, to the pain and confusion, to the weight of death staring me in the face. It torments me with a question looped on repeat: "Could you have done more to save your dad?"

I've been awakened by that same nightmare more times than I can count. I've let the "shoulds" and "if onlys" dominate too much space in my brain over the last seventeen years since my stepdad's heart attack. Even though all four arteries were at least 80% blocked, I didn't know how to let the burden go. No amount of blaming myself could bring him back, and yet, I held on. For far too long.

I've come to understand how deceiving it is to believe, even slightly, in man's ability to seize ultimate control. Dictating life and death is not up to me. The job is too big. The burden of guilt is too heavy to carry. Only God is holy enough to handle the weight. I've tried to make sense of tragedy, but I don't think I'll ever understand.

For as the heavens are higher than the earth, so are My ways higher than your ways and My thoughts higher than your thoughts.

Questioning death is a simple unassuming inquiry until you consider the source. A dark voice wanted me to question God's authority. It succeeded in planting doubt in my mind. The questions loomed over me, my mind fixed on what I could have done—accepted the help of an ambulance or driven my dad to the hospital myself. I don't know why I continued to entertain such a question. God is God. He alone has the power to determine the future. To think otherwise was ridiculous, and yet doubt continued to toy with me. The burden of guilt wouldn't let go without a fight. God could have saved my dad. *Why would He withhold His goodness?*

The Blame Game had me listing every reason my stepdad deserved to live a longer life. There was so much more for him to do:

He had just walked my little sister down the aisle.

He had three grandchildren who he adored, with two more on the way.

A new adventure awaited my parents in Louisiana.

Hadn't my mom been through enough?

The Blame Game stole years of joy from my life. It kept me blaming myself for what happened, making it impossible to see the beauty of grace around me. Thirteen years later, I finally stopped playing The Blame Game. I'd had enough. I surrendered the burden of guilt and told the spiritual darkness to leave me alone.

When doubt creeps in, the Evil One wins every time. He may not win the game in the end, but he's happy to steal my joy and peace in the moment. Complete trust in God, surrendering to the One who holds existence in His hands is our only hope. It's raising a white flag, giving up the illusion of control. Handing it over, again and again.

I've spent too much time missing grace because of a false sense of guilt. No more. There are too many beautiful lessons lying around for me to discover.

Releasing Balloons

Grace gives us courage to let go.

W e piled out of cars, all thirteen of us, for a private memorial of sorts at the lake park in my hometown. The same neighborhood lake we had walked around a gazillion times with my stepdad over the years. My mom, us four girls and our husbands, the three grandkids, and Gordy—the border collie. Sadness hung heavy but the clear blue sky begged us to reconsider.

My mom was full of energy, holding a bunch of colorful balloons with purpose spelled across her face. She always had an idea brewing, an illustration in the making, even during grief's strongest pull. Mom had planned the whole thing, leading the way across the grass near a set of brick benches along the water's edge.

Clearing her throat, Mom explained the exercise again. "Grandpa Lanny is happy in heaven with Jesus. We're going to send our balloons to Grandpa to tell him how much we love him." Her words were mostly for the grandkids, but we all needed a bit of convincing.

How do you let go of someone when everything inside wants to hold on tight?

111

Mom made her way around the circle, handing off a ribbon tied to a helium-filled balloon to each family member. My older sister, Michelle, and I, each got two—one for us and one for an unborn grandchild in tow. Even Gordy had a green balloon tied to his collar.

Dana, Brenda's youngest, looked up at her bright pink balloon. Her eyes danced as soon as her four-year-old hands gripped the curly string. She ran in circles with the ball of pink following behind her. Gasping for a breath, she asked no one in particular, "Do I *have* to let it go?"

Conner, her five-year-old big brother, started his lecture before Brenda even had the chance to explain. "Dana, the balloon isn't for you. It's for Grandpa Lanny and Jesus up in Heaven." Somehow his words must have made sense because she went along her merry way, bobbing the string up and down.

Inside, I couldn't help but agree with Dana. I didn't want to let go of my stepdad—his goofy sense of humor, his unending loyalty. The selfless kindness he showed to everyone around him made the world a better place. In all honesty, I didn't want to let go of my broken heart. I didn't want to let go of the hurt inside because in some strange way it felt good to hurt. As if the hurting was a way to hang on a little longer. Letting go felt like moving on, and I wasn't ready to move on.

The countdown began sooner than any of us wanted it to. The grandkids shouted each number out loud with Grams. "Five, four, three, two, one." Then a pause before my mom released her balloon—the first to let go. Her eyes, wild with wonder as they followed the rising ball of color into the sky. She had accepted this turn of events better than any of us could explain. Her past experiences had taught her to be open to God's redirection, to accept what comes and goes even when life is far from our original plans.

I looked side to side, everything in me not wanting to release my tight grip—on the string of the balloon or on the threads of Lanny's life that intertwined with my own. *What else could I do? Throw a tantrum and take the balloon home with me?* I figured maybe surrendering physically would help my internal heart strings to let go too.

I looked over at Josh with Tobey in his arms—they let theirs go. Michelle and Lee, Shaw and Heidi, Adam and Brenda and Conner. The orange ribbon slowly left my grip, and the pink one too. One by one the various colors reached for the sky. Even Dana released her pink sphere without a fight.

The balloons rose slowly at first, each finding its own way. Some sped ahead, others lagged before shooting up to join the rest. Isn't that how the journey of grieving goes? Each person processes on their own timetable, at their own rate.

I huddled closely with my sisters, our arms interlocked as we watched the balls of color rising higher, getting smaller by the second, our cheeks wet with tears as the tiny dots floated over a blue canvas.

We didn't speak. How could we? The fire inside our throats couldn't be quenched, not yet anyway. It would take time to articulate all the feelings inside, a different experience for each of us. We stared a bit longer, letting the reality of loss soak in deep. The seconds turned to minutes. Our eyes taking in the big blue empty sky. This was goodbye.

Letting go of grief is not an easy undertaking. I've realized it can't be planned or scripted. Helium might float away effortlessly, but grief has its own trajectory. There's no right or wrong. There's only the time it takes to accept what's happened and then believe that somehow God will walk alongside our bleeding hearts. He gives us as much time as we need.

Seventeen years has taught me a lot about grief. I didn't know then what I do now—letting go is placing the string of grief in God's hands. It's allowing Him to carry the uncontrollable heartache in this world. It felt impossible at first, as if I was dying, too. But what if letting go is a little bit of dying to myself? Dying to the grip of control that keeps me tightfisted. Dying to the illusion of life being comfortable and easy.

Releasing our balloons that day didn't mean letting go of memories. It didn't mean forgetting the unforgettable father God had blessed us with. In fact, letting go helped me to remember him more. It made talking about him easier on my broken heart.

Opening my hands, miraculously, has led to joy. It feels backward because I'd assumed joy would be required to take the first step, but it's the act of letting go, letting God hold the loose strings of my life, that has become my greatest source of joy. It's saying, "God, I trust you with my grief. I give it to you for safekeeping." When we trust God enough to be our safeguard—to lovingly hold our grief—He heals it, too.

Grief is rarely beautiful at first. It's confusing and complicated, more time consuming than I thought it would be. We may think holding onto the hurt of our past is in our best interest. But then we would never have the chance to see grace emerge from the dark places. Grace can be found in what we would never choose or want to take place. Sometimes it's physical death, and yet, the threat of relational death can be just as heartbreaking.

The letting go, the opening of hands, is where the beauty unfolds. As I muster the courage to let go, the colors fill the sky.

There's Dirt in Your Face

Grace forgives the one in the mirror.

The early fall leaves on the liquid amber hung in bright yellows and reds, with a touch of brown summer on their curled edges. I felt like the trees out my front door, top-heavy and waiting, more than tired after a long uncomfortable summer. My son, Tobey, had just celebrated his second birthday, and it wouldn't be long before the little package in my protruding pregnant belly turned him into a big brother. My energy had bottomed out weeks ago. Restless nights and endless trips to the bathroom drained my reserves, and my emotions were still raw from the passing of my stepdad. The joys of motherhood come with their share of pains.

My little boy didn't have an inkling of the past or the future, his only concern was playtime and peanut butter and jelly sandwiches—his new favorite lunch. After a morning of stacking blocks and reading board books, I couldn't take it any longer. We had to get outside where he could search for rocks and bugs, and I could relax for a few glorious minutes.

It's necessary to say that Tobey, in all his opinionated and volatile tendencies, was a darling little man. He could engage a tableful of our adult friends, leaving them in a fit of laughter at the phrases his tiny mouth formed. Articulation has always been one of Tobey's strengths, but on this particular day he didn't choose words to make himself heard.

Of the entire quarter acre lawn, he headed straight for the three-by-three-foot patch of bare ground, just to the right of the waterspout. The loose dirt combined with the right amount of water could make mud—this mom's most despised medium. After an exhausted sigh and a disguised eyeroll, I gave in and brought out his prized rotating water wheel with a red funnel on top. *What the heck, he can take a bath before lunch. Right?*

With a colorful old quilt tucked under my arm, I settled myself under the shade of our apple tree. Glancing down, I saw a dribble of leftover syrup on the lower edge of my shirt—the result of a renegade pancake. I was a mess in so many ways that morning. I rolled onto my side with a good five feet of intentional clearance from all the action. Tobey settled right in, building his surroundings into a make-shift kitchen. He waddled into the shed, retrieved a set of play dishes, and stacked them to the left of the water faucet before returning to his focused task.

After more than ample time for him to play, I dug my phone out of the back pocket of my too-tight maternity jeans to check the time. *Ten minutes until noon, perfect.* I made my way over to give Tobey a heads-up.

I'm a firm believer in the Five-Minute Warning, with a few extra minutes to spare. I learned in our Mommy & Me class that transitions are every toddler's most tantrum-evoking activity. This described my son to a T. Determined to master the meltdowns before baby number two arrived, Tobey and I had been practicing for weeks.

"Hey buddy, looking good over here. Whatcha' got cooking?"

Tobey didn't even look up at me, his focused face set on a plastic plate covered in dirt. He held it out in my direction, his two pudgy arms presented it with pride.

"Do you want a peanut butter sandwich?" He asked in his two-year-old grown-up voice.

I reached for the grubby plate, sniffing the air above the make-believe sandwich. "Oh, it smells wonderful. Did you make it for me?"

He nodded, then directed his attention to the second plastic plate.

"Hey T, you must be getting hungry. We've got five more minutes until *real* peanut butter sandwiches. Do you want strawberry jelly or grape?"

He didn't answer my question and kept right on cooking. I should have known what was coming, but I didn't suspect a thing. In my mind, the lure of gooey peanut butter and jelly would make this transition a cinch. Offering the two age-appropriate choices didn't pan out the way our Mommy & Me instructor said it would. It's funny, I figured if I parented by the book then Tobey would do exactly what the book said. Boy was I wrong.

I crouched down in a semi-squat, lower than I should have in my condition, my eyes locked with his dark chocolate beauties. He didn't flinch as his puffy little toddler hand stretched wide to grab a full palm of dry dirt. My eyes bulged. *Would he dare?* Before I could stop him, he raised his hand and released, as precise as a chef adding garlic to a skillet. Every grain of dirt launched square in my face.

He immediately knew it was trouble. He started sobbing before I could even grab his arm. I didn't have to say a thing. His time in the mud was over. As he expressed his disappointment loud and clear, I hauled his flailing filthy body over my shoulder and struggled to my feet. The blood-curdling screams pierced my eardrums, but I didn't stop our trek back to the house. My dirt-filled eyes squinted to find the back doorknob.

How in the world am I going to handle two of these little monsters?

Tobey's fists punched the air while his legs kicked wildly.

I still hadn't said a word. How could I without completely losing my cool? I had no other pressing business, but I was still too mad to think. Besides, my face was in dire need of a rinse off. When we made it to his room, I ever-so-not-gently placed Tobey in his bed, muddy shoes and all. His violent wailing muffled the sound of the door slamming shut. The screaming continued as I made my way down the hall to the bathroom.

In between sobs, he demanded, "I want my peanut butter sandwich."

Yeah right, Mister.

Cupping cool water and soaking my face, I looked up into the bathroom mirror. Leftover dirt settled in the low points of my inner ears, and the straight line of my middle part could have supplied enough dirt to plant a tree. A smear of mud ran the full length of my right hip where Tobey's sneaker had been. I replayed the last hour through my head, thinking about what I could have done differently. *There's dirt in your face. Where did you go wrong?*

I thought about my little boy, about how his whole world would soon change with a sibling entering the scene. Our precious time together was just about over. Pretty soon, there would be three of us during the day. The transition wouldn't be easy for him.

Maybe I should have entered the make-shift kitchen in all its muddy glory and completely engaged with my little cook. I wiped my face and shook my hair out over the sink. *Why didn't I?*

I could hear that Tobey had stopped crying by then, just in time for me to start. I'm convinced that pregnant tears are bigger and wetter than normal tears, and I've found the reserves are deeper, too. It dawned on me: I was in over my head. Parenting is hard. Keeping up with my son's unending energy didn't come naturally to me. The constant interaction, occasional tantrums, and bigger-than-life messes zapped every ounce of stamina I possessed. My prayers for an easy-going child had not been answered. Maybe I should have been praying for strength instead.

The toddler years required more grace than I had in me. Grace for my little man, but even more so, grace for myself. Trying to figure out how to navigate the next phase had me stumbling through every step.

In the midst of parenting Tobey, a wise mentor—a mother of four grown children—challenged me to embrace my son's humanness. To acknowledge that no matter how hard he tries to be good, he will always be an imperfect human. We're all in the same boat, parents included. She encouraged me to swap out the perfect-parent standard with a picture of love and humility—a parent who gives grace and accepts it just as readily. It's only then that we stand a chance at real connection with our kids.

Being a mother is perhaps the most humbling job on planet Earth. Over the years, I've felt as though the actions of my children is a direct reflection of my competency as a parent. It's simply not true. Two-year-olds rarely think before they act. They will need to be forgiven again and again, more times than any mother could count. They are going to mess up big-time and ironically, so will every parent willing to admit it.

Children are often a wonderfully frustrating reflection of their parents, all the qualities we fear and loathe staring back at us. The self-centeredness and lack of consideration I saw in my son was living quite comfortably in me, too. Perhaps my unreasonable demands to follow the rules were more about making my job easier, which I certainly needed. But what did he need? A little more time? A kinder mom, or one relaxed enough to remember that eventually he'd realize he was hungry, and the only "time clock" was my own. What if I'd focused on my delight in him and how love is the best teacher?

God is the only perfect parent. He extends grace to a world of people who make mistakes, who are masters at throwing tantrums. He doesn't care how dirty we are or what we've done. I'll never know what could have happened, but shame and deep guilt aren't the answers. Our failures will never disqualify us from God's unfailing love.

After eighteen years of being a mom, I'm still learning to give myself grace. Still dealing with tantrums, though they look different with teenagers. Still crying my eyes out when I know deep in my heart that I could have done better. My son isn't throwing sand anymore, but the eyerolls and heavy sighs can be just as painful. There's grace for it all. Those early tears in the bathroom mirror have made me a better mom and a more dependent child of God.

Tobey didn't get his peanut butter sandwich that day. Skipping lunch to have a long cry did us both some good. And all the released emotion of the morning contributed to a very long nap. When he woke up, chatty and pleasant, he climbed on my lap and snuggled as if nothing had happened. And I had a peanut butter sandwich all prepared, cut in half for us to share. The extra strawberry jelly oozed out with every bite, and we licked our fingers with delight.

Forgiveness for our kids is a given. The tricky part is learning to forgive the one staring back in the mirror. We need as much grace as they do.

Consider It All Joy

Grace focuses on the good.

My head throbbed as I stood over the pot of boiling water. Small bubbles began to form, the heat slowly permeating the clear liquid from the outside in. It mirrored the hopelessness invading my spirit. I didn't know how much more I could take. *Will the pain ever stop? Will the doctors ever call with my MRI results? Is this my fate forever?*

Everything in me wanted to sit down on the kitchen floor and let that noodle-water boil right over. I'd spent the day battling yet another headache. Six weeks of ice packs and Tylenol, paired with bouts of mental confusion and dizzy spells, left my body beyond exhausted. My fragile emotions hung on the edge of a steep cliff, I clawed with all my might to keep from falling.

Eight-year-old Raegan appeared at my side. She wrapped her arm around my waist and looked up with concern in her big brown eyes, "Feeling any better, Mom?"

My expression and a half-smile could have answered her question, but just then the hot water started rolling. I fumbled with the dry noodles, spilling a few over the side of the pot, entirely too close to the gas flame. "Oh, shoot! This is not going well."

Grinning, Raegan joked. "Mom, are you losing your marbles again?" A deep breath rose in my chest, I closed my eyes in frustration. The not-so-funny line my children had adopted over the mental mishaps I'd experienced in the last few months didn't strike me as funny, but how could I blame them? Most moms don't forget to pick up their kids from school or space out at traffic lights or leave the stovetop flame going all day.

I turned off the burner and laced my fingers through hers, leading her to the bottom step of the stairs. I sunk down in a heap, my head resting against my knees. Raegan brushed her small hand on my shoulder and left it there. "Mom, I have an idea."

I wiped away the tears and lifted my head. "What's that, Sweetie?"

"Your favorite things. We need to make a card with all your favorite things—like the song in *The Sound of Music*, remember?"

I felt a soft smile spread slowly across my face. We had watched the movie countless times, sang the song out loud in the car or after a hard night of homework. *How is it that our roles have reversed?* The bridge of the song came quietly at first, then resonated down the hall and into the kitchen:

"When the dogs bite, when the bees sting, when I'm feeling sad. I simply remember my favorite things and then I don't feel so bad."

Acknowledging my internal angst through the words of the familiar song helped me return to the stove and finish preparing our spaghetti dinner. A lightness grew in my spirit as I thought of my little girl ministering to me. As soon as the kids cleared the dinner plates and loaded the dishwasher, Raegan planted me at the kitchen table with her tub of markers and a blank notecard. She sat on my right side with one of her own.

"Write down all the things you love, Mom. All the things that make you the happiest. Then you can look at your card when you are sad and consider it all joy."

Dumbfounded, I asked, "Where did you learn about that?"

"Sunday school. My teacher told us we can have joy when hard times come around because God knows how to make things good. Maybe if you remember all your favorite things, it will help you believe it."

I raised my eyebrows in disbelief. *Who is this kid?* I fished through the plastic bin and found a bright orange marker.

Our colorful cards took shape, the words "Consider It All Joy" center stage while our favorite people, places, and things filled every blank space on the four-by-six inches of cardstock. She instructed me to keep my card handy so I would have it whenever I needed it. As a reminder.

The next morning, before dropping off the kids at school and heading to work, I tucked my "Consider It All Joy" card in my purse. The pain in my head lingered, but the new perspective filled my heart with gratefulness. No matter what happened, God could make it good. I had to keep believing it.

A few hours later, my cell phone began to vibrate on the edge of my desk. I glanced at the number. My doctor. The call I'd been waiting for. I stared at the screen quivering in my hand.

"Hello? Just a minute. I'm at work."

Hoping not to disrupt my coworkers, I stood up and headed for the door. I hesitated, turning back to retrieve my colorful handmade card from the front pocket of my purse. I hurried down the hallway to the break station and through the door to the balcony. I saw the parking lot below bustling with people coming and going. It seemed everyone had somewhere to go, but I stood frozen in place. My hands grew damp with nervousness. I clutched the colorful card firmly, now a bit wrinkled and moist, and lifted the phone to my ear. "Okay, I'm here."

My doctor used a flurry of terms I hadn't heard before. Confusion swept in as I stood there baffled as to what she was trying to convey. The hesitation in her voice only intensified the moment. She paused midsentence, my hope dangling on what she would say next. Erupting from the quiet, she found her resolved voice. "You have an abnormal growth in your brain. It needs to come out as soon as possible."

Even as my doctor gave me the appointment time and address of the neurosurgeon, everything melted into the background. "Wait a minute, are you saying if the growth is removed, I'll be okay?"

"Yes, but the longer we wait, the more symptoms you will experience. Once it's removed, you should be as good as gold."

Good as gold? Could I actually believe that?

I hung up and looked down at the card in my hand, at all my favorite things written in a rainbow of colors. The unknown intruder had stolen my quality of life. It had led me to the point of despair, convincing myself that chronic pain would be part of my forever future. A sliver of hope ignited my weary soul.

Raegan was right. Focusing on my favorite things, on all the good in my life, helped me to not give up. Focusing on the good is a matter of perspective. Good results and good lessons rarely look alike. Singing on steps and coloring with markers with my daughter somehow paved the way for me to discover that *good* can have a variety of meanings. During times of uncertainty gratefulness always brings about the good results God had in mind.

Even when the dogs bite.

Even when the bees sting.

Even when bad news shows up out of nowhere.

I would keep believing it. If I was ever going to get through this, I had to believe it.

Grace focuses on the good even when life feels far from good.

A Walk in the Park

*Grace delivers the peace that
passes all understanding.*

We made our way from the parking lot to the corner of the medical building. I looked up at the exterior stairwell looming before me—a flattened corkscrew wrapping up to white puffy clouds. I hoped it would be the last obstacle to solving my health crisis.

The blue California sky shone brightly, and a gentle ocean breeze refreshed my anxious spirit. A sliver of hope was all I needed. I clung to the words of a local neurosurgeon who had told me that Dr. Park was the best of the best. The only surgeon he would recommend for the job.

Josh took my arm and urged me forward. "It's on the third floor. You sure you can make it?"

My eyes softened at Josh's heartfelt concern. It's a good thing our roles weren't reversed—he epitomized the ideal caretaker. A nod of my head and we began the climb. He slowed at the first landing and looked over to see if I could go on. It felt strange to be so exhausted and shaky after being put on immediate activity suspension only a few days earlier. Breathless but determined, I kept climbing, one step at a time, holding onto his arm for balance.

"This place must have an elevator somewhere. I wonder why the receptionist told us to take the stairs."

Josh chuckled. "Maybe because she wanted you to be on solid ground. You have been a little dizzy lately."

"Like you should talk. I'm the only one here who hasn't fainted in an elevator. That was you, Mr. Lee." The playful banter took my mind off the stairs, a perfect distraction to help me conquer the second round of steps. One more hike up and a turn brought us face-to-face with a list of doctors printed on a glass door. Josh scanned the names.

"Dr. Park.... This is it."

He held the door as I made my way to the receptionist sitting behind a thick glass partition with a round opening just above her face.

She greeted me. "You must be Wendi. You're a tad early. Dr. Park is still with another patient, but I have plenty to keep you busy." I exchanged my insurance card through a cutout slot on the marble counter for a clipboard full of forms.

We weren't alone in the waiting room. Several others scrolled their phones, and one older gentleman flipped through a magazine aimlessly on the sofa across from us. I started on the paperwork while Josh checked his work email. Every few minutes, he brushed my knee lightly with his fingertips. The man glanced over and exchanged smiles with Josh.

"This must be your first visit here. The husbands are always the worriers. Don't fret. Dr. Park is an exceptional surgeon. I've spent many hours in this waiting room over the years. It gets easier." Josh and the man talked about the Santa Barbara weather for a few minutes, and I got back to work on the clipboard.

The last page, a chart-like form, had a row of printed

checkboxes on the far-right side. Each box belonged to a symptom and a blank line to record the approximate date of onset. I narrowed my eyes and read each line carefully, then paused and looked over to Josh.

"Sweetie, when did my headaches start? Seven weeks ago?"

He directed his attention back to me and slid his arm around my shoulder. "That sounds about right, just after school started back up."

I checked the box and wrote in the date. "What about the dizziness and forgetfulness?" My eyes met his and I gave him a crooked smile. "I don't know how they expect me to remember when I started losing my mind. Maybe you should be the one filling this out."

The interior office door opened. A woman in her mid-sixties emerged, relief in her eyes and a happy smile on her face. The friendly man sitting across from us jumped to his feet, took her hand in his, and they made their way to exit. He backed into the door, propping it open for his wife with the utmost care and then held it open for a nurse approaching the office with an armful of file folders.

She walked right up to us and held out her hand. "Hi Wendi. I'm Kate, your nurse navigator. How was your drive? It must have been beautiful coming down the coast this morning."

We both stood and shook her hand. I smiled nervously.

Kate appeared to be in her late twenties, tall and dark-haired, with an air of sympathy in her tone. "Let's sit down and talk about your appointment."

Returning the clipboard to my lap, I flipped through the pages. "I'm afraid the questionnaire is giving me some trouble. I can't seem to remember much of the last two months."

Kate reached out and took the clipboard, placing it on top of the file folders. She didn't even glance at the forms but met my eyes with her easygoing temperament. "No need to worry, I can fill out the rest. Tell me about yourself."

We chatted about marriage and kids, growing up, and how I had been feeling since the diagnosis. She watched my every move and asked a whole slew of questions. Her compassionate voice melted the tension in my shoulders, and I started to relax.

Before we knew it, she glanced at the clock on the wall and tucked a stray hair behind her ear. "We're just about ready to go in. I'll be with you guys the whole time. Remember, there are no silly questions. I'm here to make this as easy as possible."

The office manager escorted us to an empty exam room. Josh and Kate sat in the two chairs against the wall. I climbed onto the exam table, the thin paper crinkling underneath me. A strange image glowed on the screen of an archaic-looking monitor sitting next to a box of surgical gloves on a long counter.

A quick knock brought Dr. Park through the door, all five-foot-three-inches of him. The introductions were brief. He sat down in the only remaining chair—the one on wheels. He wore a white surgeon's coat and black-rimmed glasses. He was all business.

He enlarged the picture on the screen and pointed at a darkened oblong shape with his right index finger. "This is a tumor in the ventricles of your brain. The shaded area is a cyst, basically fluid coming from the tumor and causing some serious symptoms. This is not to be taken lightly. It needs to come out as soon as possible, to be tested. Then we can determine what's next. I recommend scheduling the surgery immediately."

Josh got a serious look on his face. "What are the risks of this kind of surgery? And why are we in such a hurry?"

I sat quietly, taking it all in while Josh asked more than a few questions. The surgery would be very invasive and require up to a year of recovery. I stared at the wall not knowing what to do or say. My mind went blank.

Dr. Park responded to every question with certainty, then took a deep solemn breath. "My surgery days are Tuesdays and Fridays. Kate, when is my next opening?"

Kate cleared her throat, "Friday morning, but next Friday is also available."

I snapped back into consciousness. "This Friday? Like three days from now Friday?" The ultimatum hit me like a club. It felt too soon. The room was quiet as my mind raced. *What if I don't wake up? What if I do wake up and don't remember anything? Three days.* I could sense my hands trying to grasp something to regain control, but there wasn't anything to hold onto.

"Next Friday would give you over a week to prepare, but I'd suggest you get on my schedule before you leave today. It can fill up quick." Dr. Park stood to his feet and shook both of our hands before leaving the room.

Josh exhaled, his breath escaping through loose, frustrated lips. He dropped his head, closed his eyes, and turned to Kate. "What if we want a second opinion?"

Kate nodded and smiled soberly. "That is entirely up to you and Wendi. There are good surgeons all over the country, and I know you want to make the best decision possible. Let's go outside. Some fresh air might do us some good."

We got up and walked down the hall, through the waiting room and out the entrance leading to the stairwell. Josh was still processing his concerns out loud when we made it to the parking lot. All the while, Kate offered her advice and a wealth of resources for us to explore.

We ignored our car and continued down the sidewalk toward the hospital as we mulled over what to do. The cement turned to the left and opened to a simple, yet quaint garden with a gravel trail and benches surrounded by beautiful tropical plants.

Kate pointed out the impressive facility in the background, but my attention was fixed on the peaceful little park. I can't explain it. The way it soothed my spirit, so green and wild against the stark white building. My head cleared, the spinning cycle of *what if* questions and *why me* anxiety came to a hush. The overwhelming fear of death or losing my memory vanished from my mind. A fuzzy kind of warmth invaded my heart, like the feeling of singing around an open campfire—like I'd be content to go on this way forever. I didn't know if I'd ever experienced "the peace that passes all understanding" before. I stood transfixed, reveling in the gift. I knew what to do.

I'd been mostly quiet, letting Josh gather the information necessary to satisfy his fix it mentality, but I needed to finally speak up. This wasn't something we could know. No amount of information or strategizing could figure out what was best for a brain tumor. Only God could truly guide us here.

I stopped walking, closed my eyelids for a moment, and took in a full breath through my nostrils. My chin, tilted upwards, soaked in the warm rays of sunshine from above. "I have something to say."

Josh stopped abruptly and put his arm around me. He waited for me to continue.

"Let's not get a second opinion. Why would we go to San Francisco or L.A. when we could be here?" I held up my arms directed at the peaceful little park. "My life is not in the hands of a surgeon. It's in the hands of Almighty God. I say we go with Dr. Park."

Josh hesitated. "Sweetie, are you sure about this?"

The questions and doubts stood still. God's peace had taken root in my heart. "Absolutely, it's going to be a walk in the park."

Josh could tell I had made up my mind. He nodded his head in acceptance and slid his hands into the back pockets of his jeans.

"Kate, how about we plan the surgery for next Friday? That gives us some time together as a family."

She smiled in approval, then opened the yellow file folder and added a note.

As we walked back to our car, energy flowed out of me. Suddenly, the world felt full of possibilities. "There's so much I want to do before surgery, so many people I want to see. You think I'll have the stamina to go trick-or-treating with the kids on Saturday? And family photos! I wonder if I can play the "brain tumor card" and get a photographer this last minute?"

My mind raced through each day of the week ahead, who I wanted to connect with, like planning a road trip with friends at every stop. I had ten full days until brain surgery. I wanted to make them the most meaningful days of my life. My once-empty glass felt fuller than it had in months.

Peace isn't something I stumbled upon. It waited for me amongst the lush leaves and blades of grass, discovering and changing my perspective in one instant rush of serenity. I'm convinced there's no man-made recipe to peace, no step-by-step instruction guide to gaining it. The peace that passes all understanding comes only from God. I've since learned it may be a slow-growing calmness or show up in a ray of sunshine at the perfect moment. But His peace enabled me to walk into the future that day with confidence. Not confidence in myself but confidence in Him.

There would be a long road ahead for us still, but with God's grace, anything—even brain surgery—can become a walk in the park.

My Best Day Ever

Grace transforms the worst
circumstances into the best outcomes.

"Wendi," a voice whispered.

A gentle touch to my shoulder and there it was again, "Wendi, it's time to wake up."

My lashes fluttered and I compelled my eyes to open. The slightest crack and then light flooded in all at once. The glare of fluorescent white burned my corneas until my squinting relaxed and the voice became a face.

A young woman, her blonde hair swept back in a messy bun, smiled down at me. Her kind blue eyes matched her shirt, and her soothing words felt like comfort from a friend I'd never met. I blinked repeatedly, trying to take in my surroundings. There was no pain or discomfort, just confusion.

"That's better, Wendi. Can you tell me your full name and age?"

I hesitated, then answered while straining to look over my shoulder—nothing but white bare walls. "Wendi Lou Lee. I'm 38." A faded green curtain outlined her silhouette.

"And where did you grow up, Wendi?"

"I was born in Los Angeles, but I've lived on the Central Coast since grade school."

She smiled patiently and held my wrist, taking my pulse. Then she pulled out a little light connected to a lanyard around her neck. She held it up to my eyes and flashed it in two quick bursts then let it fall to her chest.

"Tell me about your family."

Without a thought, I started rambling. "I've been married to my husband, Josh, for sixteen years. We have two kids. Tobey, my son, is eleven. He has the funniest sense of humor. And my daughter, Raegan, is eight. She has the most tender heart."

The young woman paused and locked eyes with mine. "Do you know where you are right now?"

My gaze traveled down from her face to a plastic name tag pinned to her shirt. *Kelly ... she looks like a Kelly.* Right above her name, an array of ocean-colored blocks—like a row of dominos in the shape of the letter C—and the words *Cottage Hospital* jumped out at me. My confusion subsided as the faint memory sharpened in an instant and all the memories of the days and weeks before rushed in. My entire lifetime flooded through my brain like a spinning film reel.

The last thing I remembered was being wheeled into the operating room, massive lights right above my head, and surgical tools spread out on a metal rolling table. Dr. Park, my surgeon, was in the corner. My hearty "Good morning!" took him off guard. He spun around with a baffled look on his face. I don't think I was supposed to still be awake. Then my world went black. I remembered it all now. *Thank you, Jesus.*

A smile spread slowly across my face. I met Kelly's baby blues and nodded. "Yes, I do. I had brain surgery this morning. I guess I woke up with all my marbles in place."

Kelly's uneasiness melted into a soft grin. "Yes, you did, Wendi, and you are going to be just fine."

Kelly pulled out my chart and started taking notes. She lifted the head of my bed with a hand-held controller and placed it on my stomach within reach. As she adjusted the thin sheet that covered me and extended the railings on the hospital bed, we kept talking. She told me I looked just like her best friend from college, that we could be twins. Whipping out her phone from the front pocket of her scrubs, she scrolled to find the picture. I chuckled at the girl in the photo. She looked like me except for the thin gap between her front teeth.

"That's impossible," I said. "I already have a twin. Her name is Brenda. We played the role of Baby Grace on *Little House on the Prairie.*"

The surprise on Kelly's face energized me and encouraged more of my story. Clearly, I was getting ahead of myself. The words that spilled out of my mouth came fast and loud. I held nothing back.

She took a step back and raised her eyebrows in shock. "You are like no patient I have ever woken up before, and it's not about you being on TV. It's something else, like your veins are full of liquid joy."

We laughed like old friends while she pushed the bed past several green-curtained recovery rooms before exiting through double swinging doors. We continued down a hallway that opened to a quad where several corridors met. To the right was a waiting room with glass windows the full length of the wall. Behind the glass, members of my family sat patiently whispering to one another. Others paced the room with worried faces. They looked exhausted, as if they had been waiting for days not hours.

It felt as though I would burst right out of my skin. I sat up, stretching to see them. Kelly noticed and slowed the bed to a stop. I took it as permission to engage.

My eyes darted back and forth in a frenzy to recognize each face and place it with the correct name. My crowded brain searched my memory banks in desperation. The newest member of the family and possibly the hardest name to recall belonged to my stepdad. He pushed open the glass door and headed straight for me.

"Hi, Curt," I said it loud and clear, almost bragging that I remembered his name. His smile exploded as he looked over to my mom and Brenda, sitting together. My eyes rested on Jen and Jodi, my friends who came with their support and giddy smiles. My husband, Josh, stopped his pacing. A spark of hope filled his tired face.

Curt grabbed my hand. "How you doing, Wen?"

It was an overwhelming question for me to answer. How do you voice so many emotions in one response? It felt impossible. I searched for the words to convey just how wonderful I really was. As the bed started to roll again, I shouted out the most absurd statement I've ever spoken.

"This is the best day of my life!"

Laughter erupted and they all took a deep breath of relief.

It's an answer that doesn't make much sense. Maybe a graduation day or a wedding day or a "birth" day, but surely not a surgery day. Brain surgery couldn't be part of anything good. Or could it?

When I saw the faces of my friends and family, love burned brighter than ever before. Waking up from surgery filled my heart with hope. I saw my life with unmatched awareness, a chance to live differently. I pledged to love deeper, to be vulnerable and honest. To serve God better and in new ways that scare me. To say the words, *I love you* more often and to more people, even when it feels a little uncomfortable.

The simple act of waking up is an unbelievable gift, after brain surgery or any day at all. My eyes could have remained closed, or my mind could have been stripped empty. No one is guaranteed eighty years or even tomorrow, but I can count on God's stead-fast love and mercy to greet me with each new day. Just as His mercies are new every morning, so is His grace.

Grace took a seemingly terrible day and turned it into the best day ever. A day that changed my perspective on living and loving. No matter how dark the future might seem, grace is the opportunity to wake up with a renewed spirit. It has the ability to transform the worst circumstances into the best outcomes. With grace, every new day has the potential to be the best day ever.

A Warm Blanket

Grace comforts us through our darkest times.

A dark-haired, partially-bald man peered through the opening of my recovery room. "Hello there, Wendi. All set for your post-surgery scan?" Armando, my transport nurse, pushed a wheelchair through the door and parked it as close to the hospital bed as possible.

"Yep, ready as ever." I swung my legs to the floor and inched my tush to the edge of the mattress. Using the metal handrail to ease my weight forward, I straightened my legs and turned to face the back wall. Armando rolled the seat edge directly against the backside of my knees as I reached down to grip the padded armrests. I lowered myself to the worn vinyl upholstery.

"The MRI is going to take about forty minutes. You want to eat a snack on the way?"

My raised eyebrows answered for me as we stopped in front of the nurse's station. "What'll it be … chocolate or vanilla?"

"Chocolate, every day of the week for me."

He handed me a white plastic spoon and opened the door of a mini fridge set under the long counter. "Looks like we're out of luck. Is vanilla okay this time?" His easy-going response and friendly smile are forever etched in my mind.

I sighed out loud, teasing him with my animated reply. "I guess it'll have to do."

I peeled back the shiny silver wrapping and plunged my spoon into the creamy pudding. The sweetness surprised me.

"Thanks, Armando. The vanilla is delightful."

Ever since waking up from surgery two days before, my senses had been at an all-time high. Even foods I didn't particularly like tasted incredible. Smells registered as either putrid or pleasantly inviting, nothing in between. Lights blinded and noises roared louder than a thousand crashing symbols. Overnight my world had become exhilarating and very uncomfortable.

Armando's caring nature eased the worries spinning through my heart with every kind word he spoke. He pushed my wheelchair down the hall to the elevators and then to the first-floor radiology wing.

The tech wasted no time at all. With the plastic headshield locked in place and the emergency help button placed firmly in my hands, the platform came to life and reeled me deep into the recesses of the machine. *Forty minutes. Just relax, Wendi.*

The typical MRI beeps and jolts commenced. I tried to do what I'd done during the other three scans—repeat my favorite Bible verse over and over again in my mind, Philippians 3:10 (AMPCE). The ritual usually calmed me down and helped the time pass.

> *For my determined purpose is that I may know Him, that I may progressively become more deeply and intimately acquainted with Him, perceiving and recognizing and understanding the wonders of His person more strongly and more clearly.*

For some reason, it wasn't working. Not this time. *God, where are you?*

My mind spiraled in fear. The thumping bore down like a

sledgehammer hitting the exterior of the gray dome. Trapped inside, yet unable to press the remote in my hand, I succumbed to a place I'd never been before. A place of sheer terror. Reason went out the window, I couldn't get a grasp on reality. It felt like those forty minutes would never end.

The platform finally emerged, dragging me with it. Tears spilled down the sides of my face, the moisture filling my ear canals. I trembled but could not speak. My gaze frozen, my smile gone.

Armando, seeing my distress, sensed trouble. He parked the chair, set the brake, and rushed over to help me. With one arm he steadied my weight, the other wrapped around my shoulder as he eased me down to rest. He stopped at a nurse's station on the first floor, picked up the phone, and requested a warm blanket be delivered right away. Then we made the long trek back to my room. In silence.

In front of the hospital bed, Armando held out his hands for me to grasp. He helped me into bed and tucked the warm blanket around my legs. A calmness came over me and my breathing slowed. He locked eyes with me and said, "It's not going to be easy, but you will get through this. Don't ever give up!"

The tears began to fall. A weak whisper escaped from my throat. "Thank you."

I learned firsthand about anxiety attacks that day. My surgeon explained later how our minds can create the illusion of excruciating pain from an overload of fear. He didn't offer me any suggestions or tips. I've had to figure that out on my own.

My life coach, Kristy, describes it this way: "If fear is walking through a dark alley, then anxiety is feeling that same fear—the terror of the unknown, the sweaty palms and racing heartbeat—while lying in your bed at home. Safe as can be." It's not a real threat. It's imagined and oftentimes fabricated by our past experiences.

I've lived through my share of anxiety attacks since then. For me, it all revolves around pain, real or imagined, and the fear of going to a place of terror again. Every person struggles with fear to some extent—even the most faith-filled follower of Jesus. No one is above it.

Scientists describe fear as one of the basic human emotions. I believe it's a survival tool, designed by God, to help us when we run into trouble. God knew from the beginning that fear would be an issue for us, maybe even the greatest obstacle to trusting Him of all.

I've been encouraged by the countless admonitions to "fear not" in the Scriptures. Depending on the translation and how loosely one counts, I've been told there are at least 365 references of the idea: "be not afraid," "be strong," "do not be dismayed," "take courage," and "fear not." In most cases, God follows up His instruction with the solution to fear—His presence. The only source to a less fearful future is God himself.

Some claim these 365 mentions are commands to follow—as if fear could be eliminated altogether. I've always thought of them more like pleadings, not reprimands. It's God's heart saying, "I'm here with you. Don't worry, I've got you. I'm going to help you get through this." He has comforted me during the darkest of times.

God's presence appears in the strangest ways when terror takes over. A warm blanket and hopeful words might seem like a small thing in the middle of an anxiety attack, but Armando made all the difference. God's grace is at work in ways I cannot even fathom, even in the words of a stranger.

No matter how traumatic my situation is. No matter how hopeless my circumstances appear to be. Even when the emergency call button is resting in my hand and fear has overtaken me. God is present. His grace shows up in the warm blanket, in the kind word of a stranger. Comforting me with the warmth of His love.

Staples

Grace wows us with the details.

M y mom emerged from the bathroom door holding a tiny bottle of hospital-approved soap, three days after being discharged. "The tub is all set. Are you ready for clean hair?"

The kids had just left for school. Josh had the day off, but Mom had come for this exact reason. I was on the couch, my legs under a cozy blanket, waiting in anticipation. Who would have thought washing my hair would bring such excitement? Without delay, I swung my feet over to meet the carpet, hesitated, and looked up at her. She helped me to a standing position and interlocked her forearm with mine to steady my weight. Guiding my feet from the carpet to the tile floor, I sighed with relief. "Thanks, Mom."

My surgeon had instructed us to wait at least seven days after my craniotomy before washing my beyond-dirty hair. I had been counting down the days and Mom volunteered to do the honors. She held my hand as I stepped out of my pajama pants, one leg at a time. Tottering like a toddler, I escaped the soft prison of flannel and stepped into the tub. I shrank down to meet the warm water, my legs as wobbly and thin as a newborn giraffe's. My mother hovered over me. *Has it really come to this? What's next, her brushing my teeth, too?*

"Oh my goodness, my legs are tiny. What happened?" I tinge of panic rose in my voice.

"They are tiny, just like when you were little. Don't worry, that's what happens when you stay in bed for a week. Everything will be okay." She smiled reassuringly and handed me a wet washcloth topped with a few drops of liquid from the tiny bottle. I dunked it into the water and moved down each twiggy leg. Mom poured water down my rounded back and ran a second soap-filled washcloth down the protruding vertebrae of my spine.

"How long before you think I'll be able to take a shower ... by myself?"

"The real issue isn't taking a shower. It's finally washing that hair of yours. You ready?"

I gave her a solemn nod and turned to face the tile wall. Mom was perched on the side of the tub, and I tilted my head back.

"How about I start with the lower section of your hair first? If everything goes well, we can finish with the surgery site."

I agreed and the hand-held shower nozzle went to work.

Mom lathered the shampoo into my long hair, steering clear of the incision. The sensation on the back of my head was glorious—the gentle pulling of hair, the fingers on my scalp. She rinsed out the shampoo, wringing the water from my soggy mane.

"Okay, up we go." My mom moved slowly, scrubbing the section of hair below my ears and inching her way closer to the eight-inch-long slice in my scalp. I held my breath.

Mom saturated my crown while gently running her fingers along the patch of shaved hair, like a headband from ear to ear. "There's still a lot of dried blood and bits of bandage. I'll try to get as much out as I can. Am I hurting you?" The concern in her voice surprised me. Mom had never been much of a nurturer.

"No, not at all. I can't feel a thing, not even the warmth of the water. How strange."

"You know what's even more strange? Seeing your scalp being held together with staples? The tiniest staples I've ever seen. All the way from end to end."

"Yea, I think Dr. Park said something about staples."

"And Wendi, you'll never believe it. There are thirteen of them."

"No way. You've got to be kidding me."

I shook my head in disbelief and turned around to face my mom. Thirteen has been a recurring number in my life—born on the thirteenth of August, the number thirteen on all my sports jerseys. I embraced the "unlucky" number at an early age and commissioned it to be my favorite number of all time. I sat there, stunned. *Thirteen staples in my head. God, You are so good to me.*

My mom's disbelief matched mine. "You know, if God knows the number of hairs on our heads, then surely, He planned the number of staples that would end up on yours. He's got you, Wendi." She leaned over the tub, our foreheads almost touching while we let the evidence of His love sink into our hearts.

In an instant, I knew I'd be okay. It didn't matter how long my recovery lasted or when I'd be able to take care of myself again. God had given me a glimpse of grace in the form of thirteen tiny metal clamps holding my scalp together. He often speaks to us in a hidden way and then waits for us to notice, like the most respectful lover. Maybe if we could only see the grace he places in every day, every moment, life could become a never-ending adventure while we wait for miracles and signs and proof. Maybe all of life is proof when we consider how absolutely everything can become evidence of grace.

The generous love of God unfolds in wildly unpredictable ways all the way down to the smallest details. Beyond what I could ever have imagined. Even God has a few favorite recurring numbers that show up again and again in Scripture. Numbers carried deep meaning in Bible times, and now God had chosen to use the number thirteen significantly in my life. Again.

It's delightful when God shows up in the small details—in something as insignificant as a number. No surgeon would have chosen thirteen staples on purpose. It's unlikely, but it doesn't matter either way because love is true and, ultimately, we won't need signs to know it. It seemed as though those thirteen staples whispered, *Don't worry, I've got this whole thing under control.*

Over the course of my life, I've seen time and time again that God chooses to reveal Himself in the trivial technicalities. To get our attention when our gaze starts falling. To grow our faith. He seems to enjoy wowing us with the smallest details. The number of our days and even the number of staples.

Brain Surgery Sitters

Grace accepts help.

"I have the next four days all lined up. Every three-hour shift is covered from nine in the morning until six." Josh looked at me with serious eyes. "Are you going to be a good patient?"

We sat at our kitchen table just eight days after brain surgery. It had been a rough adjustment coming back home: the pain still lingered in my head, bouts of dizziness and nausea upset my stomach, and the normal noise of two young children playing or arguing raged loudly inside my wounded brain. My strip of bald scalp and the row of metal staples made every interaction a little surreal. And the constipation from the pain meds, I need not expand.

More than anything, learning to sleep again was the biggest problem. Every night a replay of the day's activities and conversations looped on repeat into the wee hours of darkness. My mind reeled in frustration, I needed to sleep but couldn't. One morning around 3am, I trudged down the stairs, starving. I didn't think to be quiet or ask for help. Josh stumbled into the kitchen to find me cooking chicken on the stovetop. You could say that my decision-making skills had flown out the window. From then on, he introduced a set of post-surgery house rules for me: no being home alone and no cooking. Period.

"Your mom and Brenda can take the mornings, switching back and forth. Then I have a crew of your friends to cover the afternoons. My mom volunteered for the evening shifts. She can start dinner before I get home from work."

"Are you telling me I need a babysitter, Mr. Lee?" I cocked my head to one side and gave him a grin. "Really, Sweetie, it's not necessary."

"Yes, that's exactly what I'm saying, and it's absolutely necessary. I know it's difficult to hand over the keys to your life, but your body needs time to heal."

"How does having a babysitter help me heal? What if I promised to take it easy?" I gave him a sheepish grin.

"We all know what will happen if you're home by yourself. You'll be traipsing up and down the stairs, doing laundry. Healing is your only job right now. Two naps a day until you get back to normal at night. No exceptions, Wen. All the sitters have already agreed to mandatory rest times. You've taken care of everyone around you for years, let us take care of you."

Josh's troubled face looked older, more somber than I'd ever seen it before. He had a serious job ahead of him: organizing a calendar of brain surgery sitters while he went to work, then reigning in all my energy and stubbornness when he got home. Not to mention arranging rides to school and back for the kids, helping them with homework, and making it through the final weekend of AYSO soccer. The least I could do was roll with it. Besides, I loved the idea of friends coming for a visit, even if I wasn't too keen on having them put me down for a nap.

"Okay, okay. I get it. Who's on the list for tomorrow?"

"De is coming with her guitar, she thought it might help you fall asleep, and Rhonda will be over on Tuesday with her endless supply of essential oils."

I stared at him in disbelief, unable to vocalize my gratefulness for friends who wanted to serve me. My heart softened at the thought of it. I usually stepped in to lend a hand during times of need. It was my turn to be on the receiving end.

"Everyone wants to see you, and they keep asking what they can bring."

"Did you tell them coconut macaroons dipped in chocolate?" I laughed out loud.

"I told them their company would do you the most good."

For two weeks familiar faces knocked at my front door. Family members, friends, neighbors, mentors, and girls I had mentored. Every sitter's energetic smile made me giddy inside. I told them about my time in the hospital and showed off the thirteen staples on my scalp.

I shared with more vulnerability than ever before—about myself and about how God was teaching me to loosen my grip. To let someone else call the shots.

After our visiting hour ended, each of them ordered me upstairs to take a nap. On a few of those days, sleep came easier because of the soothing strum of a guitar or a relaxing foot rub of lavender and peppermint oil. Besides their company, people came with fresh blueberries, chocolate pudding, and yes, coconut macaroons dipped in chocolate—my post-surgery favorites. Delicious meals filled our refrigerator, and freezer, too. I received books and cozy socks in the mail, accompanied by handwritten letters to encourage me. One family came with dinner wrapped in foil and an assortment of yard tools. They mowed and edged our lawn then stayed past dark to eat with us around the table.

Every meal, every gift, every hour of time offered to us exuded love. It seemed our friends and family possessed a willingness, a yearning even, to present some small gift of service to us.

They wanted to give some insignificant token to represent the enormous weight of concern and love inside their hearts. What they gave went far beyond taco dinners and peanut butter cookies. Their presence brought a peace and calm to our household in a very traumatic time. Each gift, like a feather, collected and tucked into my pocket to savor later. The subtle awareness of beauty in the midst of pain. Evidence of joy found in the struggle.

When I think back on it, I realize my heart could have stayed hard. My stubbornness could have robbed me of the precious moments with my brain surgery sitters. I'm glad my spirit was in a place to receive their gifts of grace. The love and joy and peace they bestowed on me played a vital role in my healing. The naps helped, too. When I opened myself to the idea of accepting help, grace flooded in. Every word. Every action. Into my very soul.

Accepting help demanded a huge amount of humility. Grace to give myself a break from serving others for a change. It required an openness in my spirit to trust the people around me. To trust them to love and serve me well. And to remember that we need each other. Life is much more enjoyable with loved ones around to share it with.

Especially if they bring coconut macaroons.

The Hum of Oxygen

Grace sustains our every breath.

As leaves swirled in the late November breeze, the welcoming front porch didn't radiate its typical aura—the whole place was a hush of drawn curtains. I gave the front door a gentle tap of my knuckle and let myself in. From down the hall, my bleary-eyed, hair-tussled mother-in-law, Nani, half smiled as she trudged toward the square of ceramic tiles under my feet. She wrapped one arm around my middle and squeezed, her shoulders rising and falling with a deep sorrowful breath. Her chin quivered and those tired eyes glistened, no doubt relieved to see a friendly face. My hands overflowed with the fixings of a glorious lunch: homemade butternut squash soup, Fuyu persimmons, and chocolate. Her favorites.

Without a word, we made our way to the kitchen. Maybe she would eat and let me take a shift with the man I knew as Uncle Joey. From the looks of her, she needed a nap more than anything.

Ever since the first week of November, we didn't know if Uncle Joey would make it to Thanksgiving. Nani had brought him to their home to die. She couldn't bear the thought of him dying alone. Untreatable pancreatic cancer had taken over his body.

Joe had a few weeks at best. She had no choice but to watch her little brother grow weaker and weaker with each passing day. Cancer drained the sparkle from his eyes, the color faded as did our hope for his recovery. He knew what the future held. He wasn't scared a bit.

Surprisingly, three weeks later Joey sat next to me and nibbled on a slice of Papa Lee's BBQ turkey dipped in cranberry relish. With a loaded plate, he tried to enjoy every delicious bite without making even a dent. He continuously ooh-ed and ahh-ed about every gorgeous dish. I could tell he wanted that dinner to be as normal as possible. To laugh and share our what-you're-thankful-for moments around the table as if we all would do it again next year.

After dinner, we took a walk to the stop sign and back. Just the two of us. He held my arm and we shuffled out the door letting the soft breeze hit our faces. Our unhurried steps traveled not more than twenty yards before making a U-turn on the sidewalk. We talked about the challenges of being sick from cancer and having to rely on family for help. It had been just over a year since my surgery, but the memories were still fresh. We talked about heaven, how the view of dying is so different when you're at death's door. It doesn't seem so sad, it just is. We understood each other in that moment, more than any other time in the fifteen plus years I'd been part of the family. I'll never forget that walk with Uncle Joey, how our hearts touched and held on to each other. Those few minutes of honest conversation were the only gift he had left to give.

Thanksgiving week ended. Joe's glorious week of semi-normalcy ended right along with it. His last days proved to be harder than anyone anticipated. Especially for Nani. Delivering a nourishing meal was the least I could do.

"How's it going?" I asked as I placed the pot of soup on the back burner and gave the knob a half-turn. The flame ignited and a circle of blue gas crept over the edges of the ironclad pot. I got out a cutting board and started slicing persimmons. She sighed and pulled a chair up to the counter.

"It won't be long now. All he does is sleep. When the meds wear off, he starts groaning. It breaks my heart just watching and waiting." My mother-in-law reached into the bowl of dark orange wedges and raised the fruit to her lips. Her eyes closed in satisfaction, a deep exhale at the heavenly taste of sweetness on her tongue.

"Are you getting any sleep?" My eyebrows demanded an answer.

She wrinkled her nose and gave me a timid smirk.

"Nani, you have to sleep."

"I'm trying. The hospice nurses have been wonderful. They offer to sit with him, but I don't want to miss his last breath. His body is failing … but his heart is strong."

"What do you mean?" I stopped cutting and zeroed in on her five-foot-two-inch frame.

"He had a surge of energy yesterday. Tried to get out of bed … as if it was possible. He said, 'It's almost time to go. I have to get ready. He's waiting for me.' That was the last time he spoke."

My gaze moved to the wall behind her, still decorated with pumpkins and autumn leaves from Thanksgiving—my favorite season centered on gratitude and reminiscing on God's numerous blessings. Uncle Joe was nearing his end and wanted to be ready for heaven. The greatest blessing of all. A lump grew in my throat. The sheer innocence of the story made me smile.

I bit my lip to hold back tears and whispered, "He's ready to meet Jesus, isn't he?"

A quiet contemplation filled the room.

Nani broke the silence with a resolved tone. "And I'm ready to rest my eyes as long as you're up for sitting with him." Graceful acceptance of love is such a wonderful kind of grace.

Nani led me down the hall to the master bedroom. The steady rhythm of the oxygen machine and Joey's labored breathing greeted us. He didn't look like himself. Thinner than thin, his face sunken. Nani curled up in the corner's overstuffed chair, her head resting on a patterned pillow. "Wake me if anything changes."

Nodding, I moved the straight-backed wooden chair a little closer. Joey's thick Bible within easy reach beckoned me to read. I ran my fingers over the silver foil lettering, *Joseph Martinez*, embossed on brown leather. My lips trumpeted the worn pages of his favorite passage, Psalm 23. How fitting.

"The Lord is my shepherd; I shall not want. He makes me lie down in green pastures. He leads me beside still waters. He restores my soul."

The oxygen machine purred in the background, like an orchestra quietly setting the scene for the soloist's grand entrance. I continued, convincing but softly spoken.

"Even though I walk through the valley of the shadow of death, I will fear no evil, for you are with me; your rod and your staff, they comfort me."

At times, I stopped. *Was he holding his breath?* I couldn't hear the labored breathing. The expectant waiting ceased as Uncle Joey inhaled the seemingly rough air through his nostrils. It was hard work to keep breathing, I could tell.

"You prepare a table before me in the presence of my enemies; you anoint my head with oil; my cup overflows. Surely goodness and mercy shall follow me all the days of my life, and I shall dwell in the house of the Lord forever" (Psalm 23 ESV).

Joey struggled again, right as I finished reading. I could sense a battle inside his soul. Fighting to stay alive. A fight against death—the only obvious enemy he had left. A fight he couldn't win. And yet, death is more of a transition than an end, isn't it?

Why didn't he just let go, give up, and sprint to the house of the Lord, to the wide-open gates of eternity? Why endure the struggle with Heaven so close?

In that sweet hour, sitting next to a soul so ready for eternity yet not quite, God revealed a truth I'd never considered. Maybe Uncle Joey didn't run because he wasn't in a hurry. Maybe he wanted to praise God for a bit longer. With every labored breath. With pure oxygen going into his lungs, helping him breathe. Content to struggle, until God called him home. For some, death is the end. For others, it's just the beginning. Praising God for the rest of eternity.

Later in the pages of Scripture the psalmist also said, "Let everything that has breath praise the Lord."

Could every breath be praise? In the midst of life's challenges and the struggle to fully live surrendered to God, I pondered if every breath could contain genuine praise. What about when our conscious minds are focused on other things? Can we exhale praise without even knowing it?

To praise God with every exhale, I need grace in every inhale. Breathing in His mercy and forgiveness and steadfast love makes it possible to breathe out peace and joy and humility. How marvelous that God would create the human body to be in constant praise, to remind us that we need Him with every breath we take.

Every inhale—grace. Every exhale—praise. Is it possible to live like this, on the lookout for grace as we fight to stay alive? The possibility hinges on receiving His grace, believing His grace, seizing it in healthy doses as if our very lives depend on it. Living one day at a time with His steady presence humming in the background, sustaining our every moment. Giving us strength with his pure love.

Banana Seats

Grace overcomes fear.

It was a Tuesday afternoon in March of 2020. Josh, the kids, and I had just finished playing a game of outdoor volleyball on the back lawn—more weeds than grass and on a badminton net, but we weren't complaining. A world-wide pandemic confined most of the world to their homes and I searched for teenager-approved hobbies to fill the time. By the end of the first week, we had exhausted nearly every outdoor activity I could think of.

As Tobey and Raegan rushed inside to consume more screen-time, we folded up the net. My husband had a gleam in his eye. I could tell an idea was brewing inside his head.

"Hey sweetie, what about a bike ride with me tomorrow?"

He's a road biker—that means he shares the road with cars. I held my breath, looking from side to side. *Who me?* The excuses started lining up in my head. He'd been road biking for more than a few years by then, and my riding resume didn't feel sufficient. It included me on my cruiser traveling down paved bike paths or level sidewalk-lined streets passing cul-de-sacs and speed limit signs maxing out at twenty-five miles per hour. I tried to keep an open mind and muster a confident response.

"Sure."

It wasn't convincing, but he ran with it, and got right to work sprucing up his old road bike for me. Fear is a tame word to describe me sitting on two super skinny tires on an open road with crazy drivers whizzing by at 55mph. We live out in the country, so our version of a bike lane is the six inches between the white line and the weeds. Every left turn and swerve to avoid a pothole has the potential to end your life. I learned quickly that success hinged on knowing how and when to change gears. My first failed attempt ended with a slow walk up a steep hill.

After the humiliating walk, Josh decided a detour to the high school parking lot was in order. It's the perfect place to practice, he said. We weaved up and down the rows, under the shade of the solar panels, crossing all the empty white-lined spaces. He showed me how to quickly tap the shifter using my right index finger to gain more resistance from the highest gear to the lowest, then use a slow push and hold to go back up again. All while pedaling and steering. I'm not too proud to say it's easier than it looks. I'd never told him about the angst of my first bike riding experience, and that was on a sidewalk. We laughed as the story unfolded.

My first set of wheels boasted a bright pink frame with daisies covering the long white banana seat. The handlebars swooped up perfectly, an upside-down rainbow with silver streamers like ponytails blowing in the breeze. I was eight that Christmas morning, and it felt too good to be true.

My two sisters and I had conspired together for weeks, written letters to Santa asking for one bike to share. It sounds funny to me now, but we shared everything back then. We figured a third of a bike was better than no bike at all. I just about cried when we raced into the living room and saw not one, but *three* beauties parked in front of the brick fireplace. The twinkling lights of the

Christmas tree reflected off the shiny metal frames creating a cloud of magic sparkles dancing on the ceiling. They looked so peaceful resting on their kickstands tilted in a flawless row. I would have been happy just staring at them all day, but my sisters didn't want to waste a minute.

"Can we try before breakfast, Mom?" asked Brenda impatiently.

"It's still early, let's finish opening up the gifts and get some food in your bellies before the three of you ride off into the sunset."

Our shoulders slumped for a second, but the sweet aroma of cinnamon rolls brought a smile to our faces. We tore through the rest of our gifts and licked our plates clean before grinning at my mother, heads tilted and eyebrows raised. She shooed us down the hall to find long pants and sneakers. When I returned to the living room, my pink beauty sat all alone. Michelle and Brenda, with bikes in tow, raced out the front door.

An uneasiness grew as I walked my bike to the front porch, down the three concrete steps, and across the driveway. My left shin repeatedly banged into the plastic spikes on the pedal, confirming my fear of serious injury yet to come. My beating heart went wild, and I tightened my sweaty grip on the molded plastic handles. The closer I got to the street, the more I questioned that letter to Santa. It didn't seem like such a good idea anymore.

Michelle and Brenda were already teetering on their banana seats, with smiles spread wide across their faces, when I reached the level ground of the sidewalk. Everything in me wanted to turn back around, to sit by the fireplace and admire the bike instead of ride it.

It took every ounce of courage to swing my left leg over the bike. I stood there straddling the frame for more than a few minutes, with my rear pressed up against the tip of the banana seat. Rushing the moment wouldn't diffuse the fear I felt growing inside. I needed to give myself some time—and grace.

Just waiting and watching, I let myself take it all in. The starts and restarts, the falls of my sisters' persistent struggle. Before long, my left foot was ready, ready to pedal into the unknown. Come what may.

The sidewalk in front of our house had never been so packed, two-wheeler traffic paced back and forth all day long. I'm not sure if training wheels had been invented, but we didn't have that luxury. I wobbled and crashed again and again, not giving up until my bike cruised up and down the cracked pavement with hesitating ease. One day is all it took, but those few extra minutes of patient grace were necessary. A gentle pause paved the path to courage and determination. That night I stood taller than ever before, pride swelling in my heart as I parked my dream bike in the garage next to the cat bowl.

Practice makes perfect, or maybe I should say *nearly* perfect. No matter how many successful road rides I've completed, fear is still an issue for me. When encountering moments of personal fear, I've learned that grace is patient with me. It whispers, "You can do it," until I believe it myself and take the first step like sitting on my white banana seat on Christmas morning back in 1984.

I've found giving grace to myself in moments of uncertainty is the single best approach to battling fear. I'm able to overcome the urge to hold back when I invite patience into the situation. Breathing space won't eliminate all forms of fear, but it does provide the opportunity to take my time and proceed when ready.

How do I stand firm in the face of fear? How do I silence the doubt of the moment and my lack of confidence in what feels too hard? For me, it comes down to sifting through truth—truth about myself and truth about the power of God. When perfect

Love is all around me, my fears don't seem as frightening. I can follow God in bold and courageous ways because He'll be with me even if I fall flat on my face.

I'm slowly learning that I may never be as brave as my sisters or the man I married. I don't have to be. God gives me time and grace to be exactly who I am. He's teaching me to be brave and do hard things, but He's also giving me the space to gear up and be ready to take a step of faith. God's power is made perfect in my weaknesses, my deficiencies confirm that His strength is pulsing through me.

We will fail Him, especially when we give fear control of the handlebars. When we exchange riding through life for watching from the living room, fear wins. Every time.

Through it all, our merciful God is patient while we conquer our fears. One foot pushing down on the pedal at a time. One shaky step, one adventurous decision, one soaring bound into an unknown future. God's not in a hurry. He wants us to live fearlessly and thrive. In the meantime, He bestows more grace than we could ever imagine.

The grace to face my fears with trust in myself and my true sense of strength has never felt more purposeful than when I first decided to open my personal life to *Little House* fans all over the world. Not just going to a weekend event but sharing my everyday life. Online.

He's patiently waiting, cheering us on to rise above the fear, so that we can jump on the banana seat and ride wholeheartedly. With silver streamers celebrating.

Prayers in a Jar

Grace grows unlikely friendships.

M y eyes snapped open at the first rays of sunlight peeking through our bedroom curtains. I looked over at my husband, sound asleep with the edge of a sheet shielding his face from the growing glow of daybreak. As gingerly as possible, I crept out of bed and got dressed. My dog, Mo, heard the jingle of her leash and sprinted to the front door. I hushed her overly excited response as we escaped the sleepy house and headed to the park.

It was Thanksgiving morning of 2018. The early morning wake-up had nothing to do with stuffing a turkey or scraping together a last-minute table decoration. No, this carried much more weight than the upcoming feast. The task before me held one problem: I didn't have an inkling what I would say when my cold finger pressed the **Go Live** button for the very first time. I was terrified, but a promise is a promise.

The challenge from my conference mentor and the vow I'd made just a few weeks earlier rang in my head. "The easiest way to grow in your communication skills is to use them. Every single week. Just start with one live video."

I looked down at my workout pants and ratty sweatshirt.

Maybe I should have planned a more put-together outfit. My hair, barely brushed, and my throat feeling dryer than desert sand, I could have called the whole thing off. Mo pulled frantically on the leash, but with determination I bypassed the familiar trail and planted myself on a wood bench. Mo curled up on the grass and nibbled on a dog treat as the mental bullet points I had prepared appeared in the clear blue sky.

Here goes nothing.

The fourteen minutes on camera could have gone better. I said the word "umm" more times than I would have liked and tripped myself up at least twice, but in the end the real me showed up. I spoke from my heart and somehow managed to enjoy myself. As I pushed the red **End** button, I realized that *Little House* fans are my people. They are the crew of folks God has put in my path to love and encourage as life meanders along.

Every live video since then has been a joy, a weekly point of connection with a community of people who have one thing in common: a love for *Little House on the Prairie*. My role as Baby Grace Ingalls has given me a platform to reach these wonderful individuals who I have come to love deeply. I don't always understand why they have taken an interest in my ongoing story. Not all of them believe what I believe. And yet, they show up week after week.

My desire has always been to bring myself down from the celebrity status of a child actor and allow others to enter my world. Normal life is highly relatable. In all the typical mountain peaks and valley lows, I give them a peek into my soul. *Baby Grace in Real Life* started during that first video on Thanksgiving morning, and it has evolved over the years from building an audience to establishing deep friendships.

I'll never forget the first time I asked the people watching to pray for me. My heart was heavy, and my natural inclination went straight to the Almighty. I followed up the request with an offer to pray for them, too.

To my surprise, the prayer requests came pouring in. One by one, from all over the world. There were way too many names to keep track of in my scattered mind. *How am I ever going to pray for all these people?*

Finding an old glass milk bottle from the bottom shelf in my kitchen cupboard, I wrote every name and petition on a three-by-three-inch colorful square of paper and prayed specifically for each request. My prayer jar took residence in the living room, next to an antique iron dish drainer used as a catch-all for bills, magazines, and Christmas cards. Whenever I saw the jar, it reminded me to pray.

I realized early on that I wouldn't be able to remember every name and situation, but God remembers them all. *God, I pray for each person, every request in this jar. God, do your thing, act on their behalf as You see fit.* The glass jar filled up faster than sand through a sieve. It wasn't big enough. I needed another.

Now, years later, I have several glass jars tucked in corners and on shelves in every room of my house—reminders to pray for my tribe of *Little House* fans. It's part of my daily routine, an honor to pray for them as they continue to pray for me. The give-and-take goes back and forth and our hearts are intertwined forever.

The most amazing thing happens when I hear back from some sweet soul, telling me how God heard our prayers, how He came through to save or comfort or heal. Sometimes the miracle is a teenager's softened heart or a loved one's glorious trip to Heaven.

These answered prayers are deposited into the biggest jar I could find: a globe of glass with a tiny three-inch opening on top—my faithfulness jar.

As the faithfulness jar fills up, one miracle at a time, I'm overwhelmed by our generous God. Awestruck at how He loves us and is constantly working in our lives. I see a connection deepening with people He has brought into my life in the most bizarre way. Through Facebook of all places.

If you told me five years ago that a social media platform could be the vehicle to making meaningful friendships, I would have laughed out loud. But God truly brings people together, in person and online. He links past experiences and present longings to create future friendships.

My life wouldn't be the same without the *Little House* community that has evolved since 2018. They know all about me, my biggest joys and deepest fears. I know their names and their stories. We communicate like dear friends. When I see my faithfulness jar filling up, it's a visual reminder to keep praying for them.

Some of my beloved audience I've met at *Little House* events over the years and then our friendship continued: Barnaby, Eric, Shelli, Jayne, Elizabeth, Kristi, and Sally. The list could go on and on. Fans who have become friends. I've hugged them in parks and gymnasiums, exchanged Christmas cards, spoken at some of their churches, shared meals together during airport layovers, and even experienced a Broadway show together in a London theater.

But most of my fans-turned-friends, I've never met face-to-face—like Margaret from Scotland. She often wakes up in the middle of the night on the other side of the world to watch my live videos. She prays fervent prayers on my behalf. She isn't any less of a friend, and one day I'll finally meet Margaret. Maybe she will show me around Scotland, or maybe Heaven.

It's all grace when I look at my life and what I believe God has called me to do. To serve a community of people—*Little House* fans. People who are uniquely positioned in my sphere of influence. I conquered my fear and found a community of effer-vescent joy that holds each others' hearts across time and space. It's a ministry I've given my life to. These fans-turned-friends are some of the sweetest red tail feathers of grace I've ever collected. They burn bright against the shrubbery of life, in all its ups and downs, filling me with joy.

A Note from Wendi

———

T hrough these chapters, I've looked back at the moments
that shaped my life, tried to give you an up-close seat to
all I've experienced—the good and the bad and everything
in-between. It wasn't a painless endeavor. I doubt revisiting the
ghosts in your closet ever is. The one common denominator in
every moment is the beauty of grace revealed in so many different ways, definitions that go beyond our preconceived boundar-
ies of what grace means. Some are wildly obvious while others
don't make a lick of sense unless you've lived through a similar
experience. The challenge is to see grace with new eyes, a dare
to discover it in the everyday moments of our lives.

How many stories of grace do you have emerging from your
heart at this very moment? What will you find when you dig
through your highest of highs and lowest of lows? I invite you
to participate in this dare, the dare to discover God's match-
less grace tucked among the thorns and leaves of your past. I've
found His grace is bigger than we could ever comprehend. So
enveloping and bright. And yet, these feathers of grace get lost
unless we open wide our eyes to see them.

There's a collection of red tail feathers within your reach. I
hope you'll join me in recognizing the beauty of grace all around
us. I'd love to hear what you're finding, online or in person,
wherever our paths may cross.

Stories of Grace

I've collected stories from a few of my friends—their stories of grace—to share with you. Some of them are *Little House* fans and others I rub shoulders with every day. They are people I've met along the way who have experienced God's grace in a unique way. As I did with them, I challenge you to discover the beauty of grace within your own story.

Meet Susan.

A wife, mom, and avid tennis player until her spine collapsed and grace took on new meaning.

After a healthy sixty years of living, Susan woke up one morning and couldn't lift her head—her spine was collapsing without reason. This atypical spinal condition has led to fourteen major surgeries in twelve years. The life she enjoyed living disappeared in a moment.

With the third failed attempt to surgically implant rods to strengthen her spine, the rods broke. Susan did too. Depression set in. Twice she lined up her medications and took them all in one gulp. By the grace of God, His plans outweighed hers.

Susan spent a full year in an assisted living care facility to help heal her spirit. She learned about meditation and journaling, and how to give herself grace to endure living with a disability. Playing tennis and sailing with her husband of thirty-eight years is how she imagined spending their time during retirement. Instead, Susan is mostly confined to the lower level of their home in constant pain. Her disability makes even reaching for a mug in the cupboard nearly impossible. She uses a walker for stability and her husband is an expert at lacing her shoes.

Susan and her husband watch tennis tournaments on TV and enjoy ocean drives to see the waves crash on the shore. Susan knows that time is short, and their time together is a gift. The help she requires will only increase, and soon her husband won't be physically able to provide the care she needs. For Susan, observing his sacrificial service is a reflection of God's steadfast love—a heart-gripping beautiful expression that I have had the pleasure to behold. An expression of grace right before my eyes.

How would you define grace?

"Grace has to do with giving. God giving to me so that I can pass it along to others. It's a feeling of comfort, of joy. Realizing that with God beside me everything I have is enough."

Where have you seen grace at work in your life?

"Grace came to me in a place, a place to heal so that I could return home to my family. It came from an understanding husband who has shouldered so much for me. And from God who has given me the ability to be content … on most days, and His power to renew my heart."

Meet Sally.

*She got another chance at love
when Howard walked into her life.*

The first time Sally saw Howard, he held a Bible in his hands and wore a smile on his face. That image paints the perfect description of Howard—devoted to the Lord and always brightening someone's day. He not only loved Sally but became a father to her two teenagers, Mark and Sarah. Howard modeled a life of faith, trusting and loving God and encouraging others to do the same.

After fourteen years with the love of her life, Sally began a different phase of togetherness when Howard got sick with hepatic liver encephalopathy—the diagnosis results in the loss of brain function when a damaged liver doesn't remove toxins from the blood. It looks like dementia that comes and goes.

Sally became Howard's full-time caretaker for seven years until hospice stepped in to help. It was an emotional rollercoaster, never knowing if Howard would recognize her or know what year it was—day to day that changed depending on the toxin levels. Her once vibrant and helpful husband needed Sally every waking moment until God called him home.

Howard is gone now, he's dancing on streets of gold, free from pain and mental confusion. Sally is learning that grief isn't always about tears. Sometimes it's watching Howard's favorite show or enjoying a bowl of Cheeto Puffs—Howard's favorite snack. God had been preparing Sally for this stage of life, a life without Howard, for years. Losing someone you love is always hard—but grace shows up for Sally every day.

How would you define grace?
"Grace is receiving an outpouring of God's favor and out of the overflow I can give it to others."

Where have you seen grace at work in your life?
"God's grace covered me with wisdom and the ability to care for Howard when I didn't feel qualified to make the appropriate medical decisions that were needed, especially in the last two weeks of his life. Grace embodied the hospice team who helped

me physically care for Howard and emotionally care for myself when it all felt too hard."

Meet Sam.

At thirty-two years old, a battle with
Triple Negative Breast Cancer made her faith soar.

The diagnosis: a rare and very aggressive form of cancer that requires more chemo and has a much higher reoccurrence rate in the first five years compared to most cancer cases. At the time of her diagnosis, Sam's twin boys had just turned seven and her daughter was only three. The pain and uncertainty seemed more than she could bear. Waves of gut-clenching fear crashed all around. She remembers calling her husband at the firehouse where he worked, crying for hours and asking him, "What will happen to the kids if I die?"

Fear of the unknown sparked Sam to start a "Miracles" journal, believing that God is a miracle worker. Every time she felt God's presence or heard His voice, every verse that jumped off the page, she wrote it down. The miracle is that God used the journal to combat Sam's fear. It drew her to the Comforter anytime fear came rushing in. That's what happens when our eyes are searching for grace—we find it. Her countenance changed from grasping control to giving it up.

Sam had a double mastectomy, followed by sixteen chemo treatments. She no longer fears what will happen to her children if cancer returns. Her job is to teach and show her children how to deal with trauma and where to turn when bad things happen. People around her commented on her strength. Sam's response, "No, I'm weak, but I have a very strong God."

One of the most difficult times was losing her hair, not only for herself but the kids. She didn't recognize the hairless head in the mirror. She felt like an alien in her own body. To the kids, a bald mom was a constant reminder of cancer. They preferred she cover it up. Sam decided to have a little fun with it and bought three wigs—one of them was pink!

How would you define grace?

"God giving an undeserved, intense, miraculous comfort and ability to withstand trials. I can confidently say that my strength and ability to withstand everything that came with breast cancer most definitely did not come from me."

Where have you seen grace at work in your life?

"I felt God's living presence so intensely at times that it would take my breath away. There were moments that I could say I heard His voice. And my ridiculously funny husband taking me to every chemo treatment. I didn't need someone to commiserate with me, I needed someone who could make me laugh over the silliest things. He did that for me."

Meet Ofrah.

*As a missionary kid in an emotionally abusive home,
she found hope in a violin.*

Ofrah's unstable family, brimming with continuous fighting and blame, resulted in a confusing childhood. On the outside, her father was a lay preacher to farm workers in South Africa, but their homelife told another story. Her young faith didn't know how to navigate the mixed messages and lies that permeated her world. She grew up with a weight far too heavy for a girl to carry.

At sixteen, just after her father left, Ofrah's world began to fall apart. She felt unwanted, unnecessary, and unloved. Her schoolwork suffered and she didn't have the energy to get out of bed. She blamed herself for every setback, convinced that she had messed up again, until a stranger gave her an unexpected gift—a violin. Ofrah had dreamed of playing the violin as a very young child, and now God had made that dream a possibility. Holding the violin gave her hope to carry on.

Realizing that this one gift could have only come from God, Ofrah's broken spirit was renewed. She hungered to know God in a deeper way and joined an online discipleship ministry for young adults during the pandemic. Through regular Zoom meetings she learned that God had made her for a purpose. Her depressed state of mind and suicidal thoughts lost their power. With every move of the bow, Ofrah felt God's presence. He changed everything for Ofrah—how she viewed herself and what she believed. Her purpose continues as she and her mother hope to start a healing center for women recovering from toxic relationships to help others find hope through Jesus.

Grace rarely looks the same. For Ofrah, grace presented itself through unexpected people pouring into her, encouraging her to never give up—to keep living. Through music, especially the melodies she plays on her new musical instrument. It came through a restored relationship with her mom and through God's gift of eternal life. A gift that won't ever be taken away.

How would you define grace?
"Grace is God's kindness. Small gestures of love that add up to an overwhelming sense of being valued just as I am."

Where have you seen grace at work in your life?
"His grace has shown up for me in small ways—through people mostly and a musical instrument. I believe if we take the time to notice the seemingly small gifts, then these things will change our lives. I know grace has changed mine."

Meet Bill.

Loneliness overwhelmed him until
God gave him a new family to love.

Cancer, heart disease, and complications from diabetes took the lives of Bill's immediate family. His mother, father, and younger brother gone—too soon. He was alone, devastated and grieved by extreme loneliness. At times, he wanted to leave this earth and join his beloved family in heaven. Birthday celebrations, vacations, and treasured holidays became the worst days of the year because Bill had no one to spend them with. No one to call family.

That all changed when a friendly lady named Jenny visited a home improvement store where Bill worked. A remodel of her home meant house projects galore. Jenny was there buying drywall, electrical outlets, and paint supplies almost every day. Their friendship grew with every visit. And one day, Jenny invited Bill to join her family for Thanksgiving dinner.

It was difficult for Bill to accept that first invitation. He felt like an outsider, an intruder of sacred family connection around the table. After much persistence and patience from Jenny, he accepted and showed up with a Dutch apple pie, feeling like a stranger crashing a family reunion. The hospitality of Jenny and her sister melted his fears away. That warm family feeling, a feeling he had been missing, filled his heart with hope.

One holiday turned into another and now Bill is part of a new family, a family that loves and supports him like his birth family did. They don't share a lifetime of memories—not yet—but with each passing year love and loyalty grows. Most families begin by saying vows or in a delivery room. Bill's started by loading drywall. That's unthinkable grace.

How would you define grace?
"Grace is found in the everyday little things of life as much as the

big things. Seeing the first robin of spring, hearing crickets on a late summer evening, or a child's laughter playing at the park. It's all part of God's handiwork in our lifetime of experiences, no matter how seemingly small or insignificant."

Where have you seen grace at work in your life?

"God's grace is the calming feeling I receive during unexpected complications with my health. His presence in my life is grace, giving me perseverance and peace. He gives me tools to battle depression and the courage to embrace a new loving family. Because of God's grace I'm never alone, and that is the greatest gift of all."

Meet Kacie.

After a fire consumed her home,
grace shifted her perspective on what truly matters.

On a cold blizzardy morning in South Dakota, flames engulfed Kacie and Joe's historic country home. They got out just in time, along with their one-year-old daughter and Daisy the dog who was hiding behind the couch. Everything else burned to the ground. Gone in a matter of minutes.

Kacie remembers driving away in utter shock, her baby strapped in the car seat and the clothes on her back reeking of smoke—the only possessions she had left. She walked the aisles of Walmart in a mess of tears, unable to process what had happened and why. She left with the necessities: diapers, dog food, and a sweatshirt. And then it hit her—all the things that really mattered were safe. Everything else could be replaced.

It was a shift of perspective for Kacie. A lesson in trusting God to provide for them, recognizing that the things of this world won't matter when we get to eternity. We can't take them with us anyway. How we live our lives, loving and giving glory to God, is what we take with us. One of Kacie's favorite passages is found in Ecclesiastes because everything we do "under the sun" apart from God is meaningless. That's a whole lot of stuff.

People rallied around Kacie and Joe, grace put into action from their friends and family, and even strangers. They generously provided food and furniture, monetary gifts, and even helped them paint their rebuilt home that they moved into less than a year later. I've been in their home, it's a haven of grace and hospitality. Just inside the front door is a sign that reads, Rise and Shine & Give God the Glory. It's a constant reminder to Kacie and an appropriate response to every gift he gives us. Even if the gift means losing something we love.

How would you define grace?

"Grace is the ultimate form of love and forgiveness, the greatest blessing from God given to us—sinners who are given so much."

Where have you seen grace at work in your life?

"Grace shows up every single day, in big ways and small ways. The more I recognize how much grace God gives, the more I am inclined to show grace to others through compassion, love, and forgiveness. A kind gesture may have more of an impact than you know."

Meet Elizabeth.

*Widowed and left to raise her teenage boys alone,
she felt God's presence stronger than ever.*

Elizabeth's world shattered when her husband of twenty-five years never made it home from a trip to see the Northern Lights. One slip led to a fall. He was found days later. Her initial feelings of shock turned to dread at the thought of going through life without him, of parenting her boys without their father.

With so many decisions to make and no strength left within, Elizabeth turned to the loving support system around her. Her extended family, church family, friends and coworkers became God's hands and feet to help fill the gap. Her brother-in-law stepped in and took care of the financial aspects. Her sons started meeting with a counselor. She joined an online Bible study for young Christian widows, attended a GriefShare program, and received valuable help from a grief expert.

Life trudged on with work and school. Elizabeth's broken heart didn't know how to move forward without her loving husband. It felt impossible, and yet God showed up again and again. From people's generous gifts to songs declaring God's faithfulness to personal notes her husband had written before his passing. Every tiny evidence of grace came together and proved His love for her. When life began to unravel, God was an ever-present comfort to Elizabeth, giving her the strength to be a comfort to her boys.

Elizabeth and her sons' hearts will never be the same. One can't just get over losing a husband or a father. The journey of grief is unknown, but the hope of heaven is certain.

How would you define grace?
"Grace is when God continually seeks out opportunities to show up and support us, reminding us that He is faithful. Even when He feels far away, He's not."

Where have you seen grace at work in your life?
"When I'm looking for it, I see God's grace at work in my life in the seemingly small things that now seem so big. A supportive family, our last memories together, and God's voice through song."

Meet Heidi.

*A stay-at-home mom gave the gift of motherhood
to another through surrogacy.*

With two wild boys of her own, my little sister, Heidi had her
hands full when the first serious thought of surrogacy went
through her mind. She wanted to continue the legacy of loving
God and loving people that my stepdad had instilled in us when
he was alive. Being blessed with easy pregnancies, Heidi hoped
to give the gift of motherhood to someone who otherwise would
never experience it.

She was drawn to one couple's story in particular and the journey began. After scores of appointments and one failed transfer,
Heidi and the new parents saw a tiny heartbeat flickering on the
ultrasound machine.

All was progressing seamlessly until Covid arrived and the
country shutdown. Heidi, at thirty-six weeks along, abandoned
her big plans of daily swimming at the gym and attending a yo-
ga-for-pregnancy class. Instead, she became a homeschool teacher overnight with her protruding belly along for the ride, avoiding the grocery stores and the news.

Surrogate birthing protocols changed weekly due to the pandemic adding to the stress and unknowns of labor and delivery.
It all worked out in the end with little Lucy's parents arriving
just five minutes after she made her entrance into the world. It
gave Heidi a few precious moments to hold Lucy before handing
the miraculous bundle to an overjoyed new mother.

When love abounds, grace follows. Out of the abundance of
love she had received, Heidi sacrificed to make another mother's
impossible dream of a family come true. Giving the gift of grace
in the form of a child is beyond beautiful, a demonstration of
love through action.

How would you define grace?

"To me grace is loving and accepting others even when you don't know someone's past circumstances. God has given each of us so much grace and loves us anyway. How can we not extend a fraction of that grace to others?"

Where have you seen grace at work in your life?

"Being a mom of two wild boys in today's world is exhausting. I give and receive grace daily. My kids can be button-pushers, sneaky eaters, and screen obsessed selfish little beings. Aren't we all? I strive for the fruits of the Spirit—that love, joy, peace, patience, kindness, goodness, faithfulness, gentleness, and self-control would permeate my days."

Thank You Notes

———

Thank you to Josh—my husband. I'm so glad God sent us a little bird with red tail feathers. You have been with me for the whole messy, wonderful journey. I love you.

Thanks to T&R. You two are the best kiddos ever. I love how my weaknesses have developed strength and independence in you. I'm proud of the people you are becoming.

Thanks to Jackie—my mom. You have come through again, helping me to recreate the stories of my childhood.

Thank you to Karen—my writing partner. Your friendship, writing deadlines, and grammatical expertise have been invaluable. This book contains my bruised, battered, and at times bleeding heart—your hands are covered in red.

Thank you to my Writing Girls. It takes a healthy dose of support to live out our callings as writers. Thank you to Holly, Nicole, Carrie, Shauna, and Lisa.

Thank you to Mick Silva—my editor. For silencing the other voices and encouraging me to write the book I dreamed of writing, the book inside my heart. I am forever grateful for the way you gently shaped these chapters and challenged me to go a little bit deeper.

Thank you to my family of Little House cast members—especially Alison Arngrim (also known as "Nasty Nellie Oleson"), Charlotte Stewart (Miss Beadle), and Pam Roylance (Sarah Carter). Your unending love and support have blown me away. Can't wait for our next adventure together.

Thanks to You—my readers. You are the reason I wrote this book. Now go discover a few red tail feathers of your own.

Wendi's First Book

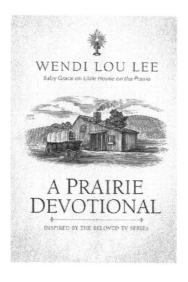

Available wherever books are sold or visit https://wendiloulee.com to purchase signed copies.

Your book review matters because it helps Wendi connect with more people. It is the best way to show your support. If you enjoyed this book or Wendi's devotional, please leave a review on the platform you purchased it from. If you purchased a signed copy from Wendi personally, please leave a review on Goodreads. https://www.goodreads.com/

Wendi Lou Lee is a follower of Jesus, a former child actor, and author of *A Prairie Devotional*. The four seasons she spent on *Little House on the Prairie* playing Baby Grace Ingalls are among God's greatest blessings. In 2015, Wendi was diagnosed with a brain tumor that changed the direction and purpose of her life. Her surgery and recovery led to a newfound freedom: sharing her story of God's goodness through life's most difficult circumstances. Connecting with people—one person at a time—brings Wendi the most joy. Wendi, her husband, and their two teenagers call the Central Coast of California their home. When Wendi isn't hanging out with *Little House* fans or writing about her adventures, you can find her paddle boarding at the beach or walking their Bernedoodle—Mo.

How To Connect
with Wendi

Visit her website: https://wendiloulee.com/

- Order autographed books
- Submit a speaking request
- Send Wendi a message on the Connect Page
- Sign up for Wendi's newsletter list – When you do, you'll get a bonus chapter from *Red Tail Feathers* as well as Wendi's "10 Not-So-Secret Baby Grace Facts Sheet."

On Facebook: https://www.facebook.com/wendiloulee13

- To connect with Wendi and join her weekly live videos visit her public Facebook page: Wendi Lou Lee as Baby Grace
- To participate in an intimate community of love and support check out Wendi's private group on Facebook: BIG-time Grace

On Instagram: @wendiloulee

- Follow along on Wendi's travels, sharing her stories of grace. See the red tail feathers Wendi continues to collect wherever she goes.

Made in the USA
Monee, IL
27 September 2024

66716320R00105